Thank you for choosing a SAGE product!
If you have any comment, observation or feedback,
I would like to personally hear from you.
Please write to me at **contactceo@sagepub.in**

Vivek Mehra, Managing Director and CEO, SAGE India.

Bulk Sales

SAGE India offers special discounts
for purchase of books in bulk.
We also make available special imprints
and excerpts from our books on demand.

For orders and enquiries, write to us at

Marketing Department
SAGE Publications India Pvt Ltd
B1/I-1, Mohan Cooperative Industrial Area
Mathura Road, Post Bag 7
New Delhi 110044, India

E-mail us at **marketing@sagepub.in**

Get to know more about SAGE

Be invited to SAGE events, get on our mailing list.
Write today to **marketing@sagepub.in**

This book is also available as an e-book.

Road to Rights

Copyright © Programme on Women's Economic, Social and Cultural Rights, 2016

All rights reserved. No part of this book may be reproduced or utilized in any form or by any means, electronic or mechanical, including photocopying, recording, or by any information storage or retrieval system, without permission in writing from the publisher.

First published in 2016 by

SAGE Publications India Pvt Ltd
B1/I-1 Mohan Cooperative Industrial Area,
Mathura Road, New Delhi 110 044, India
www.sagepub.in

YODA Press
268 AC Vasant Kunj
New Delhi 110070
www.yodapress.co.in

SAGE Publications Inc
2455 Teller Road
Thousand Oaks, California 91320, USA

SAGE Publications Ltd
1 Oliver's Yard, 55 City Road
London EC1Y 1SP, United Kingdom

SAGE Publications Asia-Pacific Pte Ltd
3 Church Street
#10-04 Samsung Hub
Singapore 049483

Published by Vivek Mehra for SAGE Publications India Pvt Ltd and printed at Saurabh Printers Pvt Ltd, Greater Noida.

Library of Congress Cataloging-in-Publication Data Available

ISBN: 978-93-515-0914-1 (HB)

Road to Rights

Women, Social Security and Protection in India

Edited by
PRITI DAROOKA

Contents

Preface	vii
Priti Darooka	
Acknowledgements	xvii
Introduction	1
Dr. N.C. Saxena	

CONCEPTUAL FRAMEWORK

A Society Which Cares: A framework for universal social protection	21
Harsh Mander	
Unpacking Social Protection from a Women's Rights Lens	32
Sejal Dand	
The Human Right to Social Protection and the Post-2015 Development Agenda	40
Dr. Timo Voipio	

MISSING DIMENSION

Social Protection for Women Workers: With special reference to unpaid domestic workers	61
Indira Hirway	

Women's Invisibility as Workers 71
    Aasha Kapur Mehta

Livelihood Security Critical for Women's Social Security 90
    Nalini Nayak

Unpacking Social Security

Social Pensions: The real Aadhar for the Niradhar 101
    Anjor Bhaskar

Our Secure Beliefs and their Insecure Lives: 130
Sex workers organize for change
    Shubha Chacko, Gowri Vijayakumar and
    Subadra Panchanadeswaran

Food and Nutrition Security in India: Challenges ahead 147
    Biraj Patnaik

Maternity Entitlements in India: An overview 168
    Yamini Atmavilas

Strengthening NREGA from a Gender Perspective: 194
Learnings from the field
    Subhalakshmi Nandi

Women and Social Security: Convergence model 208
of delivery
    Rashmi Singh

About the Editor and Contributors 225

About PWESCR 229

Preface

Social security is an investment in building a nation that is just and humane. It is an investment in human resources, which can provide overall security for a person within the family, workplace and society. Social security includes measures designed to ensure that everyone has an adequate standard of living, including basic needs such as adequate nutrition, housing, education, healthcare, clean water and sanitation, required to live a life with dignity. It provides a safety net from contingencies and risks that impact a person's ability to provide for themselves and their families. These contingencies include illness, disability, accidents (injury), death, unemployment, pregnancy, child care, widowhood, old age, and violence/conflict. Apart from an extension of these basic measures and services, social security also includes protection of livelihoods by providing access, control, management and ownership of productive resources to women and by guaranteeing just and favorable conditions of work for all. The right to social security thus represents an important human right and an essential precondition for the realization of all other human rights. It represents an essential transformation from needs-based charity to rights-based social justice.

With a comprehensive introduction by Dr. N.C. Saxena, the book is primarily divided into three major sections. The first section looks at the conceptual framework in social security; the second discusses the missing dimensions of social security and protection for women in India from a feminist perspective; and the third is on unpacking social security by exploring experiences and lessons learned from various interventions on the ground. The authors discuss social protection measures in India and their limitations, and suggest remedial action. The book aims to understand the current situation, trends and potential of social protection programs for women in India, and reviews the impact of several sectoral programs, such as the Mahatma Gandhi National Rural Employment Guarantee Act (MGNREGA), social pensions and maternity benefits. It also studies the problems faced by specific vulnerable groups, such as female domestic workers and sex workers.

The introduction highlights the fact that the social sector in India is starved of funds. The overall expenditure on this sector is constrained by the low tax collection, as the Tax to GDP ratio in India is merely about 16–17%. According to Dr. Saxena, this is the main reason why investment in health and education in India does not reach the level of other middle-income countries. Although 70–80% of the total expenditure on the social sector is borne by the states, they have not been able to arrest the decline in social expenditure as a proportion of their total expenditure. Some of the main social protection programmes that are not performing require a basic change in their design at the central level in order to ensure better delivery at the state level. Dr. Saxena also tries to draw the attention of readers towards two issues pertaining to women's empowerment: their falling share in work participation, and lack of ownership rights on agricultural land, despite legislative measures taken in 2005.

Harsh Mander, in 'A Society Which Cares: A framework for universal social protection', mentions three major streams of discourse around the broad idea of social protection across the world. One is a kind of risks-related discourse, which takes as its starting point the axiomatic desirability of globalized market-led economic policies. It acknowledges that there are cycles in market capitalism, and that people need to be protected from the rigors and suffering imposed by the downward phases of these cycles. The second stream derives from some notion of the basic needs of all human beings, and the duty of a welfare state to provision these basic needs to all citizens. The third is one of human rights discourse, and it begins from the conviction that all persons have some intrinsic human rights. It is the state's duty to ensure that all these human rights are adequately realized, either by directly provisioning them or by creating a regulatory or facilitating regime, which ensures the supply of and access to all of these rights. Harsh contends that the discourse in India on social protection has actually been centred on three categories or streams: insurance (life, disability and health insurance), pensions for workers in the unrecognized sector and a range of unconditional cash transfers. Taking into account the diverse streams of discussion around social protection in India, there is a need for a more carefully grounded gendered understanding.

In 'Unpacking Social Protection from a Women's Rights Lens', Sejal Dand argues that the social protection measures currently in place do not account for the multiple vulnerabilities faced by women. We have to recognize the specific vulnerabilities of various groups, deconstruct the mechanisms of exclusion to ensure that the universal right to social protection accords primacy to the principle of automatic inclusion of those who are most vulnerable to exclusion. Experiences of organizing women through the formation of groups, unions, federations, and community-based organizations shows that these enhance the voice and agency of women to engage with institutions of community/state, which, in turn, affects the ability of women to negotiate social relations within the household. This material investment and support for women's organizations has to be made an integral part of the social protection floor. Otherwise, it will be impossible to challenge the underlying patriarchies embedded in the institutions of family, community, state and market.

Timo Voipio, in 'The Human Right to Social Protection and the Post-2015 Development Agenda', makes four points, on rights, inequalities, inclusion and care. Global coalitions of international agencies, governments and social partners are today united in advocating inter-governmental normative resolutions that place the idea of social protection floors right at the center of the global post-2015 agenda of rights-based, inclusive, inequality-reducing sustainable development. Drawing on Finland's experiences, Voipio discusses how gender equality has always been an essential element in the country's transformative social and economic policies, as it consciously strives towards achieving a 'Society for All', inclusive of all women and men, girls and boys. Besides human rights and social justice reasons there have been strong economic motivations for Finland's inclusive and equality-oriented policies. The realization that inequalities create social conflicts, which lead to a waste of economic opportunities, is significant. Voipio argues that social protection systems will never succeed without the critically important contributions of professionally competent and motivated professionals of care, i.e. social workers. One of the best ways to empower women and to enable them to move forward in their working careers is to formalize and professionalize care work.

Indira Hirway, in 'Social Protection for Women Workers: With special reference to unpaid domestic workers', says that the concept of social security has expanded radically in terms of its content and coverage during the past few decades. Social security needs of men and women are different. The assumption that taking care of a household automatically includes all the members of the household is no more acceptable. There are no gender neutral policies, and therefore, the social security of women is to be viewed independently and separately. It is important to treat unpaid service work as part of economic work. Unpaid workers, who are mainly women, suffer from a large number of vulnerabilities. These need to be addressed through a set of suitable social security measures. While arguing that the unequal distribution of unpaid (and paid) work between men and women is at the root of all pervasive gender inequalities and the unequal power relationship between men and women, Hirway also points out that social security measures cannot go all the way to address gender equality and empowerment of unpaid women workers. The purview of macro-economics needs to be expanded to incorporate unpaid work.

Aasha Kapur Mehta, in 'Women's Invisibility as Workers', contends that there are serious inaccuracies in the recording of work contributed by women in India. She highlights three issues in the context of the invisibility of such work: under-reporting or non-reporting of women's work, thereby rendering it invisible; deviations between the National Sample Survey (NSS) estimates presented in the reports on key indicators of employment and unemployment in India and other documents based on these surveys and the NSS Report on Participation of Women in Specified Activities along with Domestic Duties, 2009–10; and unpaid care work that is neither recognized nor included in estimates of GDP. There are serious inaccuracies and a measurement failure in the recording of contributions made by women through the work they do. The NSS uses activity codes for determining which activities are to be counted as work and which are not. Mehta says that for the contribution of women as workers to become truly visible, it is important that NSS take the logical step and include the responses to its probing questions in the field while estimating the worker population ratio (WPR) for women presented in all the reports on key indicators of employment and unemployment in India and other documents based on these surveys.

In 'Livelihood Security: Critical for Women's Social Security',

Nalini Nayak focuses on what social security means for poor women workers, small women producers who live at the margins, but who are critical in providing not only the subsistence base to over 50% of our population, but in creating a social matrix of harmony. The chapter examines the livelihood security of these millions of small producers, even subsistence producers, who form an important spoke in the economic wheel, and who are mostly women. At the outset, Nayak posits three key questions: What does subsistence mean? Why is it important to safeguard subsistence? And what does social security for subsistence producers imply? Social protection or security is a right of communities and should figure high on any democratic agenda. The government should make a commitment towards securing their livelihoods and providing the wherewithal for developing them in terms of adding value and making them sustainable.

Anjor Bhaskar, in 'Social Pensions: The real Aadhar for the Niradhar' discusses the National Social Assistance Programme (NSAP), which caters to the needs of some of the most vulnerable sections of our society that desperately need support—widows, the elderly and disabled, and those who have lost the earning member/s of their family. NSAP assumes massive importance as it is the only national-level policy to provide income support to these highly vulnerable groups of people, many of whom would otherwise be on the brink of starvation and destitution. The findings of this chapter have been enriched by a study conducted by the Indian Institute of Technology (IIT), Delhi, called the Public Evaluation of Entitlement Programmes (PEEP) Survey. The findings pertaining to the implementation of the pension programs bring to light the way forward for the program.

Shubha Chacko, Gowri Vijayakumar and Subadra Panchanadeswaran, in their chapter 'Our Secure Beliefs and Their Insecure Lives: Sex workers organize for change', discuss how sex workers' access to social security hinges on their relationship to the state. According to the authors, (re) considering them as workers is a significant conceptual and practical shift as it brings issues such as work conditions, social protection and security, voice and participation rights to the policy table. For those in the informal sector across identities and divides, recognition of their work, which is their livelihood, imparts a sense of dignity and an identity of great value to them. The authors suggest a roadmap for what needs to be done to improve the conditions in which sex workers live and work.

Biraj Patnaik, in his chapter on 'Food and Nutrition Security in India: The challenges ahead', states that India seems to have prospered, but Indians clearly have not. In 2001, the Indian government had a surplus food grain stock of 60 million tonnes; however, a large number of hunger deaths were periodically reported from across the country. He contends that the status of nutritional surveillance remains abysmally poor despite India possessing a robust statistical infrastructure on all other fronts. On the positive side, the National Food Security Act, 2013 has made specific provisions for maternity entitlements and for ration cards to be issued in the name of women. In the absence of more concrete measures to address the structural issues related to gender discrimination in India, this would, however, remain a tokenism.

Yamini Atmavilas, in 'Maternity Entitlements in India: An overview', looks at how maternity entitlements bring together economic and social, productive and reproductive, and medical and social aspects. Arguing for more broad-based maternity entitlements and protection in India, Atmavilas discusses three key framing contextual realities with respect to maternity and maternity entitlements in the country. There is a real need for evolving frameworks that balance universal coverage with enough attention to, and provision for the particular, while recognizing the individual needs of different groups of women, gender norms and disparities, and economic and contextual realities.

In 'Strengthening NREGA from a Gender Perspective:

Learnings from the field', Subhalakshmi Nandi proposes that the Mahatma Gandhi National Rural Employment Guarantee Act (MGNREGA) has created a legal and institutional basis for the right to work, rights at work, right to wage parity, minimum wage, backed by strong accountability mechanisms, and is also beginning to inspire a longer-term vision of reviving the agriculture sector through the building of assets for rural communities and supporting their livelihoods. Based on these experiences and learnings, she suggests the a bottom-up paradigm, with a rights-based approach and the empowerment process at its core in order to achieve the desired outcomes of making gender equality a reality. From a gender perspective, therefore, the learning is that rights and empowerment complement each other, and for this, organizing women, building their networks and institutions, dialoging with social movements, and increasing their voice and agency have to urgently become part of the discourse on social protection in India.

Rashmi Singh, in 'Women and Social Security: Convergence model of delivery', presents a convergent mode of delivery, starting from measures for convergence at the level of planning and implementation for maximum impact of social protection schemes. There has been an increasing recognition that concrete measures are needed to create synergies for improving the quality of outcomes. It has been understood that in order to address women's needs holistically and across sectors, not only is the design and delivery of a program important but also how the inter-linkages are conceptualized at the outset. Institutions play a very important role in making such convergence efforts possible. These institutional mechanisms can manifest themselves in either co-location of services or single-window facilitation points through which access can be improved to different services spread across different service providers. The single-window approach minimizes the time and energy required on the part of those entitled to access social security measures. The Convergence model has proved its relevance as an efficient approach at the policy level and an effective delivery mechanism for social protection in both rural and urban settings. The biggest learning from the Convergence model has been that when women become prime movers for their own development.

One of the first comprehensive source books on social security, *Road to Rights* will be of immense value to governments, policy makers, development sector workers, and academics. The book draws immense learning from extensive field studies, social science insights and policy studies. It provides good reference material for researchers and academics interested in social protection and gender issues. Even though the case studies presented are mostly from India, the lessons and experiences, and the recommendations for social protection interventions hold significance to many countries, especially those in the global South, which face similar kinds of challenges.

Priti Darooka
Founder and Executive Director
PWESCR

Acknowledgements

This book has been inspired by discussions at the Conference on Women's Social Security and Protection in India, held on 6–7 May 2013 at the Indian Social Institute, New Delhi. The conference was convened by PWESCR in collaboration with UN Women, Heinrich Böll Foundation, ILO and the University of New South Wales (UNSW). Its main objective was to identify and unpack various perspectives on the issue of social security for women in India by bringing together a diverse range of participants from the government, trade unions, women's organizations and UN agencies on a common platform. It was thus a step towards ensuring that women's voices are heard, and their real-life situations understood, when challenges relating to their social security and protection are being addressed.

PWESCR duly acknowledges the support from Subhalakshmi Nandi (UN Women Office for India, Bhutan, Maldives and Sri Lanka) and Dr. Axel Harneit-Sievers (Country Director for Heinrich Böll Foundation's India Office) for the publication of this book.

Anil Kumar (Manager, Research and Advocacy, PWESCR) has also contributed in organizing the chapters and coordinating in the various stages of the publication of the book.

Introduction

Social Protection Programs and Women in India

Dr. N.C. Saxena

Social protection programs have a long and chequered history in India. These were taken up even in the colonial period as test works in famine-hit areas, but became a more regular feature with the rural employment programs initiated in the 1970s in drought-affected regions, with a view to save the poor from starvation. Gradually, rural employment programs such as the National Rural Employment Programme (NREP) and Jawahar Rozgar Yojana (JRY) were extended to the entire country as a poverty reduction strategy. Similarly, the supply of subsidized food that was primarily meant for the urban population, in order to control food inflation up to the 1980s, was gradually extended to rural areas. Social pensions were introduced in the late 1990s by the central government in India as a 'safety net' to target those who are not likely to benefit from growth-oriented productive activities, such as persons with disabilities, poor older persons, pregnant and lactating mothers. Thus such programs have had multiple objectives: to save the vulnerable from extreme distress, to reduce poverty, and to extend welfare to those unreached by the market.

During the last 10 years the Indian government has converted many welfare programs into entitlements by passing suitable legislations, such as the Mahatma Gandhi National Rural Employment Guarantee Act (MGNREGA), 2005 and the National Food Security Act (NFSA), 2013. These were part of the post-2004 Congress-led government's rights-based development strategy, actualized through a series of laws, including the Right to Information, Right to Education, Right to Public Services, and Forest Rights Act, besides MGNREGA and NFSA.

The chapters of this book discuss social protection measures in India, their limitations, and suggest remedial action, primarily from women's point of view. The book aims to understand the current situation, trends and potential of social protection programs for women in India, and reviews the impact of several sectoral programs, such as MGNREGA, social pensions, and maternity benefits. It also studies the problems faced by some specific groups, such as female domestic workers and sex workers, from a human rights perspective.

One of the first source books on this subject, it is going to be of immense value to state governments, field workers, policy makers, donors and NGOs. It is a rare combination of extensive field study, social science insights and policy studies, and should be good reference material for researchers and academics interested in social protection and gender issues. Even though the book discusses case studies mostly from India, the experiences gained in the process are of significance to many developing countries that face similar kinds of challenges.

My task in this introduction is not to summarize these excellent chapters but to express my own thoughts about the three most important social protection programs: MGNREGA, the provision of subsidized food through the Public Distribution System (PDS), and the Integrated Child Development Services (ICDS) Scheme. I have tried to draw the attention of readers towards two issues pertaining to women's empowerment—their falling share in work participation, and lack of ownership rights on agricultural land, despite the legislation to this effect in 2005.

THE SOCIAL SECTOR IS STARVED OF FUNDS

Although central allocation for programs in the social sector has gone up by almost 10 times in the last decade (at current prices), part of the increase is illusory because the Pay Commission Award has added to the salary burden. Thus the budget increase may not have resulted in a corresponding increase in the number of teachers or doctors. Second, 70–80% of the total expenditure on the social sector is borne by the states, but they have not been able to arrest the decline in social expenditure as a proportion of their total expenditure. It is likely that as the Government of India stepped up its share in social sector expenditure, states decided to cut down on the plan schemes that they were supporting. This process may be somewhat reversed from the 2015–16 budget onwards, as the central government has reduced plan transfers to the states meant for centrally sponsored programs by about Rs. 60,000 crore and expects the states to bear the additional burden from the enhanced devolution of central funds as recommended by the XIV Finance Commission.

THE LOW TAX BASE IMPINGES ON SOCIAL SPENDING

The overall expenditure on the social sector is constrained by the low tax collection, as the Tax: GDP ratio in India is just about 16–17%, as opposed to 31% in South Africa, 32% in Russia, and 34% in Brazil.[1] This is the main reason why investment in health and education in India does not reach the level of other middle-income countries. According to the Economic Survey

---

[1] International Monetary Fund (2011), *Revenue Mobilization in Developing Countries.*

2013, the total expenditure (plan and non-plan) on education and health by the centre and the state governments combined as a percentage of GDP has only been around 3% and 1.2%, respectively, as against the global norm of 6% and 3%. Poor revenues do not permit the government to substantially enhance financial allocations for the social sector.

In addition, some of the main social protection programs are not doing well, as discussed below. These require a basic change in their design at the level of the central government as well as better delivery at the state level.

MGNREGA

MGNREGA does not work well in many of the poorer states, such as Bihar, Odisha, Assam and Uttar Pradesh, and hence its impact on poverty reduction has been marginal. Out of about a crore poor rural households in Bihar, only 20 lakh got work in 2012–13, and that too only for about 35 days in a year; the rest 80 lakh did not get work even for a single day. This is notwithstanding the fact that another one crore (who are just marginally above the poverty line) would have willingly worked, had work been available. On the other hand, in Tamil Nadu the number of rural poor households is only 16 lakh, but 71 lakh found work under MGNREGA in 2012–13. Expenditure in Bihar on the scheme in 2014–15 was Rs. 1,076 crore, and in Tamil Nadu it was Rs. 3,916 crore. Richer states are doing better than poorer states at creating jobs. It makes no sense to run the program in the labor scarce districts of Kerala, Punjab, Haryana, Himachal Pradesh and the north-east. On the other hand, the upper limit of guaranteed work should be enhanced from 100 to 150 days per household in the poorest 200 districts, with monitoring of assets such as ponds, bunds, check dams and planted saplings for at least five years.

Moreover, a large number of studies on MGNREGA have pointed out the following weaknesses in the program:

- Falling financial allocation and job creation over the years
- High percentage of incomplete works
- The objective of drought-proofing is not being achieved
- Delays in wage payment
- Non-payment of unemployment allowance
- Inadequate monitoring and third party assessments

The stated objective of the scheme is to accomplish drought-proofing, and increase agricultural production on marginal holdings, especially in semi-arid regions and uplands, but the sustainability and productivity of assets created is never monitored, with the result that the program is reduced to creating short-term unproductive employment with no focus on asset creation or soil and water conservation. Its impact on agriculture may even be negative, as alleged by the Ministry of Agriculture.

Decline in Wages at Constant Prices

Rural wages at current prices saw an average annual growth of a mere 2.9% in 2014–15, which is much below the rise in consumer prices.[2] This needs to be compared with the rise in such wages by 15–20% per annum during 2009–12. Three factors seem responsible for the trend: moderate increase in support prices of crops, recession in real estate business leading to a slump in construction activities, and a drop in employment guarantee expenditure due to reduced fund allocation for MGNREGA from 2014–15 onwards. The central government has also directed states not to grant bonuses on procurement of wheat

---

[2] http://www.businesstoday.in/current/economy-politics/not-so-acche-din-for-rural-wages-in-india/story/214378.html

and paddy as that distorts market prices and adds to inflation. From October 2015 onwards, rice will not be purchased from millers at the support price, and these changes in policy may further dampen both agricultural production and rural wages.

Food Security

According to the latest Global Hunger Report, India continues to be in the category of nations where hunger levels are 'alarming'. National Sample Survey Organisation (NSSO) data shows that the cereal intake of the bottom 20% in rural India is only 10 kg per month as against 12 kg for the top decile of the rural population, though the poor need more cereals as they engage in more manual work, and their access to expensive fruits, vegetables, poultry, and milk is negligible. With their limited resources the poor are forced to spend more on health, children's education, transport and fuel than before. Food is required but is not demanded from the market due to lack of resources, leading to a greater number of poor being undernourished. Endemic hunger continues to afflict a large proportion of the Indian population.

There are also issues at the macro-level. According to the central government's Economic Survey 2014–15, food grain production in India went down from 208 kg per annum per capita in 1996–97 to 200 kg in 2011–12, which was a year of bumper production. Despite the reduced production, India has almost doubled its stocks in government godowns and, in addition, has been exporting[3] an average 7 million tonnes of cereals per annum, causing availability to decline further, from

---

[3] The policy regarding export of cereals should be revisited. If basmati rice is to be exported, an equal quantity of ordinary rice must be imported. It is highly unethical to export food grains when our own people are suffering from starvation.

510 gm per day per capita in 1991 to 439 gm in 2012. This has adversely affected the open market price as also the cereal intake of the bottom 30%, and has increased hunger levels in India.

The National Food Security Act, 2013 promises to cover about 18 crore households, as opposed to only 10 crores before the Act. However, till September 2015 only 13 states had been declared as eligible for coverage under the Act. No new state has been added since March 2014, with the result that the total annual offtake of food grains under the Public Distribution System (PDS) has remained unchanged at about 45 million tonnes in the last three years. Had all states been covered the annual offtake would have been around 60 million tonnes.

All is not well with the PDS in India. Weaknesses in the distribution system include ration cards being mortgaged to ration shop owners, large errors of exclusion of BPL families, prevalence of ghost cards, with weaknesses in the delivery mechanism leading to large-scale leakages and diversion of subsidized grains to markets and unintended beneficiaries. Fortunately, some recent attempts have been made by states to improve the PDS. It had always worked quite well in Tamil Nadu, Kerala, Himachal Pradesh and Andhra Pradesh, but now states like Chhattisgarh, Odisha and Rajasthan have undertaken state-level PDS reforms by extending coverage, improving delivery and increasing transparency.

REDUCING CORRUPTION THROUGH DIRECT BENEFITS TRANSFER

The Government launched the Direct Cash Transfer scheme on 1 January 2013 to transfer cash into the bank accounts of beneficiaries across 20 districts in the country. The scheme has now been rechristened as Direct Benefits Transfer (DBT) and covers seven welfare schemes. The money is directly transferred into the bank accounts of beneficiaries who have Aadhaar

(UID[4]) cards. LPG and kerosene subsidies, pension payments, scholarships and employment guarantee scheme payments as well as benefits under other government welfare programs are being made available directly to beneficiaries.

Unlike other welfare schemes launched so far by the centre, DBT helps in timely and quick transfer to intended beneficiaries. The direct transfer of cash into the account of the targeted beneficiary is a winning proposition for the recipients as it aims to eliminate the dual pricing system (the main reason for leakages) in various government-sponsored welfare schemes and subsidized food, fuel and fertilizer schemes. It is expected to infuse financial inclusion on a greater scale in rural India.

It may, however, be added that the large-scale substitution of PDS by direct cash transfers (DCT) is not feasible, as food grains purchased from farmers through the Minimum Support Price (MSP) mechanism need an outlet for distribution. Introducing DCT nationally would mean that the government would have to end the state procurement regime. That is neither politically feasible nor can it be in the realm of consideration by any government in India, given that more than 60% of the population is still dependent on agriculture. At best, DCT could be tried on a pilot basis in a few poor localities of metropolitan cities, as is being done in Delhi.

DBT, however, is different. Under this program, the entitlement holders would still buy their food rations from Fair Price Shops (FPS) as they do now, with the difference that they now submit their biometric details to the FPS owner through a point-of-sale device that is connected either via a GSM network or through other means to an integrated stock-management system.

---

[4] Unique Identification Number, later renamed as Aadhaar number, an initiative of the Unique Identification Authority of India of the Indian government to create a unique identity for every Indian resident.

The government should abolish the dual pricing system and sell stocks to the FPS dealer at market price, say Rs. 20 for wheat. The consumer would go to the dealer with only Rs. 2 in cash, as before, along with her/his UID card to buy a kg of wheat, and the remaining Rs 18 would be transferred to the dealer through the card. This will vastly reduce leakages and subsidy as well as improve the dealer's attitude towards the buyer. As of now the dealer avoids the consumer as his main interest is in selling the grain in the open market. Once he is given grain at market price, he would be forced to welcome the card holder and persuade her/him to come to his shop at the earliest so that the transfer of subsidy can take place.

This would not only ensure that the right people get their rations, but would also free entitlement holders to buy their rations from any FPS and not be tied to a single vendor. In other words, it would ensure 'entitlement portability', which will allow PDS entitlements to be accessed anywhere in the country, and greatly help the poor migrant workers, who are presently unable to access their entitlements. This would revolutionize the PDS by providing genuine choices to entitlement holders. It would also significantly help reduce corruption.

ICDS

The main program to address malnutrition of women and children, Integrated Child Development Services (ICDS) is being run through some 13.5 lakh centres, called Anganwadi Centres[5] (AWCs), covering 102 million beneficiaries under supplementary nutrition (SN), which includes 83 million children below six years of age and 19 million pregnant and lactating mothers. However, the program is doing quite

---

[5] These are generally one- or two-room structures where children gather for about four hours every morning for various ICDS activities.

poorly. A comprehensive evaluation of ICDS by the Planning Commission concluded that only 19% of the mothers reported that the AWC provides nutrition counseling to parents. More than 40% of the funds meant for SN are being siphoned off. A mere 31% children receive SN and 12% children receive it regularly. Only 38% of pregnant women and lactating mothers, and 10% of adolescent girls receive SN.

Another evaluation of ICDS by the National Human Rights Commission shows that despite Supreme Court orders to provide hot cooked meals, all centres in Gorakhpur, Uttar Pradesh supply only packaged ready-to-eat food, containing merely 100 calories, as against a norm of 500 calories, and 63% of food and funds are being misappropriated. The food being unpalatable, half of it ends up as cattle feed.

The Comptroller and Auditor General of India's (CAG) performance audit[6] in 2013 revealed how ICDS was failing to help infants and young children. The audit, covering the period 2006–07 to 2010–11, found a 33–45% gap between eligible beneficiaries and actual recipients of SN. CAG also confirmed that the sub-standard food being distributed was unpalatable.

THE NEED FOR CHANGE IN THE ICDS DESIGN

ICDS has not yet succeeded in making a significant dent in reducing child malnutrition, as the program has placed priority on food supplementation rather than on nutrition and health education interventions, and targets children mostly above the age of three when malnutrition has already set in. Very little of the ICDS resources, in terms of funds and staff time, are spent on the under-three child, and this low priority must be reversed.

---

[6] http://articles.timesofindia.indiatimes.com/2013-03-06/india/37499356_1_cag-audit-icds-malnourished-children and http://zeenews.india.com/news/nation/substandard-food-being-distributed-by-anganwadis_834305.html

Therefore, the focus of the ICDS programme should be on components that directly address the most important causes of under-nutrition in India, specifically improving mothers' feeding and caring behaviour, improving household water and sanitation, strengthening referrals to the health system and providing micronutrients. The basic nature of the program should be altered from being centre-based to outreach-based, as the under-three child cannot walk to the centre and has to be reached at his/her home. Another advantage of visiting homes is that the entire family, not just the mothers, can be sensitized and counseled.

The need to discourage 'ready-to-eat' food in Supplementary Nutrition Provisioning

The Government of India should discourage the distribution of manufactured 'ready-to-eat' food, as it leads to grand corruption at the ministerial level. Unfortunately, however, it has only encouraged such tendering by laying down the minimum nutritional norms for 'take-home rations' (a permissible alternative to cooked meals for young children), including micronutrient fortification, thus providing a dangerous foothold for food manufacturers and contractors, who are constantly trying to invade child nutrition program for profit making purposes. ICDS should learn from the success of mid-day meal programmes that provide hot freshly cooked food and have been operating fairly smoothly even in states not known for efficiency, whereas the packaged food supplied in ICDS even in efficient states is not popular with the children, besides its supply being irregular, and local participants being discouraged.

Gender Issues

Despite India's remarkable economic growth over the past two decades the progress in achieving gender equality and women's empowerment has been unsatisfactory so far. The ratio of females to males in 2011 for the age group 0–6 was 914 to 1000, which is the lowest since 1947. The literacy rate among females aged 7 and above has certainly increased from 54% in 2001 to 65% in 2011, but it is still 17 points less than for men. Gender inequalities are reflected in the country's human development ranking: India ranks 113 of 157 countries in the Gender-related Development Index. More than 90% of women continue to struggle in the informal/unorganized sector with no legislative safeguards.

The prevailing social constraints of patriarchy largely relegate women to the inside sphere. Added to this are the dual responsibilities of women being tagged with heavy work responsibilities in agriculture, animal husbandry and other traditional sectors, which create a syndrome of gender stereotypes, marginalization, alienation and deprivation of women in the informal sector. Even when their hard work produces surplus they do not generally control its disposal, which has traditionally been and continues to be men's domain.

Women's Unrecognized Workload

While women in India have always worked harder than men, their role as workers has not been fully recognized by planners and policy makers. According to the 68th Round NSSO survey, for the age group 15–59 years, the Work Participation Rate[7] (WPR) at the all-India level in 2011–12 was only 26% for females and 84% for males.[8] The reasons for the under-reporting of women as workers are many: women's work is often

---

[7] This covers both the employed and those who are unemployed but looking for work.

[8] National Sample Survey Organisation (68th Round) (2011–12), Key Indicators of Employment and Unemployment in India.

informal, unpaid and home-based; it is flexible, non-standard and considered an extension of domestic work and, therefore, frequently indistinguishable from it. Greater gender sensitivity is needed to correctly appreciate and record the productive nature of women's work.

In addition to under-reporting, what is even more alarming is the fact that WPR for females has been consistently going down since 1983, as shown below (based on various NSSO reports).

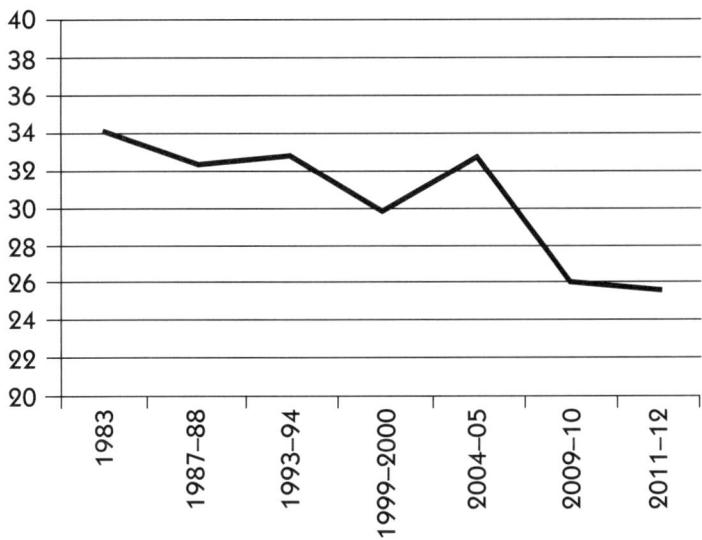

Figure 1: Changes in female WPR (% of women in work force)

The decline in the number of female workers is a matter of concern as it increases their dependency on men and thus strengthens patriarchal norms.

There could be many explanations for the fall in the number of women workers in the last 30 years. First, the number of women students in the age group 15–25 has increased and therefore these women are not in the labor market. Second, as prosperity increases there is a tendency in Indian households to withdraw women from work outside their homes. Households where women don't perform manual work outside the home are viewed as having a higher status than those with working women due to the perception that poor women work only because they have no choice. The proportion of working women declines as we move up the caste hierarchy.

Third, rural women are being displaced by growing mechanization. Farmers in Punjab are switching to mechanical rice transplanters, and the use of combine harvesters is spreading in Bihar. Fourth, minor forest products that women used to collect are disappearing, as the preferred forest policy is now becoming more timber oriented. Finally, non-farm jobs such as those in construction, retail trade and the hospitality sector are largely male oriented. These tend to be some distance away from the village where men can go on a bicycle, while most rural women do not know how to ride a bicycle.

In addition to an increasing dependency ratio, the NSSO data shows two other trends as regards women's role in agriculture. First, among the rural women who have been classified as workers, a greater proportion work in agriculture when compared with men, as relatively few women work in the more productive non-farm sector; and second, women's share in the total number of agricultural workers is increasing over time, leading to their greater involvement in agriculture. As men migrate to urban areas and to non-farm sectors in response to both the distress in agriculture and in search of better job opportunities elsewhere, women's responsibility both as workers and as farm managers has been growing, leading to an increasing feminization of agriculture.

OWNERSHIP OF LAND

Ownership of land, however, continues to be concentrated mostly in male hands in our patriarchal society. It has been estimated by Bina Agarwal that in India, land ownership in favor of women is not more than 2%. Lack of entitlement to land (and other assets such as house, livestock, and so on) is a severe impediment to efficiency in agriculture for women cultivators because in the absence of titles, women cannot get credit or be entitled to irrigation and other inputs, especially technology. In addition to improved production, the clinching argument in favor of land titles to women is the stability and security it provides, the protection it affords from marital violence, and the bargaining power it gives women in household decision making and in the labor market for wages. Without title to land, women are not recognized, even by the state, as clients for extension services or as candidates for membership in institutions such as co-operative societies.

Before 1956 devolution of both acquired and inherited property was governed by the personal laws of the community. Although equal rights were granted to women in acquiring property through the Hindu Succession Act of 1956, rights to inherited agricultural land were specifically exempted from the Act, and were made subject to the tenancy and land reform laws of the states. According to the tenurial laws of Haryana, Himachal Pradesh, Jammu and Kashmir, Punjab, Delhi and Uttar Pradesh, the specified rules of devolution show a strong preference for agnatic succession, with a priority for agnatic males.

CHANGES IN 2005

Little effort was made until 2005 to do away with these discriminatory laws. Finally after 50 years of the 1956 Hindu Succession Act, the government addressed some persisting gender inequalities in the Act by bringing in the Hindu Succession (Amendment) Act, 2005. The 2005 Act brings all agricultural land on par with other property and makes Hindu women's inheritance rights with respect to land legally equal to men's rights across states, overriding any inconsistent state law. This can potentially benefit millions of women who depend on agriculture for survival. However, neither the Department of Land Resources, Government of India, nor the Ministry of Women and Child Development has issued a single circular asking the states to implement the law. The result is that antiwomen laws and practices merrily continue in the states.

Even though the law has been amended in favor of women, they themselves often forgo their claims to garner support from their natal family in anticipation of marital discord or dispute, even though such support may not actually materialize. Women also face impediments in operationalizing the statutory codes and getting their names included in the records. Also, ownership does not always translate into control, as is the experience of matrilineal societies of Meghalaya where control is exercised by the maternal uncle. Decision-making in cropping patterns, sale, mortgage and the purchase of land or the instruments of production remains in the hands of the men of the household.

Thus the issue is not only legal, it is also cultural. As women's control over loans, income and assets goes down, their access to social resources such as knowledge, power and prestige diminishes. Disparities in gender status are intensified with the emergence and deepening of other forms of stratification. Subordination and seclusion of women is more noticeable in communities where social differentiation and hierarchy based on ownership patterns or on prestige are more pronounced.

Finally, equal pay for equal work is one of the cornerstones of the gender equality movement the world over. But the Labour Bureau data shows there has been little progress in terms of parity of salaries for men and women for equivalent work in India. Even more alarming is the fact that even though wage disparities have always existed in rural parts of the country, in some spheres of activity, the divide has widened. So while men were paid 70% higher wages than women for ploughing work at the end of 2004–05, the difference rose to 80.4% at the end of March 2012 and stood at 93.6% at the beginning of 2013–14.[9]

Along with creation of new jobs the government should also aim at improving the quality of employment in the unorganized sector which is where nearly 92% of the workforce is engaged. Workers in the unorganized sector do not have the benefit of several laws, such as the Minimum Wages Act or the Factories Act. They are also not covered by statutory welfare measures such as maternity benefits, provident fund, gratuity, etc., all of which were put in place after intense struggles by the Indian working class in the pre- as well as post-Independence period. Many self-employed persons like vendors, ragpickers, and petty traders make their services available from the early hours of the morning to late at night, despite all kinds of inhospitable working conditions, including hostility from police and municipal authorities.

It is hoped that this book will sensitize policy makers to these issues, and greater justice will be done to workers in the informal sector, particularly women.

---

[9] http://www.thehindubusinessline.com/economy/in-rural-india-gender-equality-in-wages-is-still-a-distant-dream/article4915110.ece

CONCEPTUAL FRAMEWORK

A Society Which Cares
A framework for universal social protection

Harsh Mander[*]

Speaking of social protection, I am reminded of Noam Chomsky's luminous words. He observed that the idea of social protection is basically the idea that we should take care of each other. I think this summarizes as well as can be the idea of social protection, and it underlines what we easily forget: that policies of social protection are embedded deeply within the larger overarching ethic of social solidarity. He, however, goes on to caution that we live in times where this is considered a dangerous, subversive idea that must be crushed at all costs. I think that this rejection of the conviction of our mutual responsibility to each other, including those who are weaker, in difficulty or in need, is really the heart of our failures in extending universal and adequate social protection, and we need to recognize and address this.

When you look at the literature over the decades and across countries—both academic and policy literature—at times one finds a large number of terms used interchangeably or in overlapping ways, and in other instances, the same words

[*] This paper is based on a presentation by Harsh Mander, at a National Conference organized by PWESCR between 6–7 May 2013, in New Delhi.

meaning quite different things to different people. We talk about social security, social protection, social assistance, social insurance and social welfare, and there are also other variations of this. So, I think that the one thing we need to be clear about, for ourselves, is to define what we are talking about when we talk of social protection and social security. What specifically are we talking about in the context of India? And finally, how should this discourse be made more relevant for women? I will make some brief suggestions for each of these questions.

Many Ways of Understanding Social Protection

Scanning the literature, I find that globally there are at least three major streams of discourse around the broad idea of social protection. One is a kind of risks-related discourse. This takes as its starting point the axiomatic desirability of the globalized market-led economic policies. It acknowledges that there are cycles in market capitalism and that people need to be protected from the rigours and suffering imposed by the downward phases of these cycles. Sometimes there is an acknowledgement that even in the upper crests of the cycle, you might still have some people facing disempowerment and suffering. This is seen as a somewhat unfortunate by-product of otherwise desirable sets of economic policies. So, this risk model of social protection, where we are looking at side-effects and cyclical elements of market-led economic growth, attempts to protect people from these unfortunate side-effects of essentially benign economic and social policies embedded in the primacy of private markets.

There is a second stream in the discourse that derives from some notion of the basic needs of all human beings, and the duty of a welfare state to provision these basic needs to all citizens. These ideas, coming out of a 'basic needs' discourse, have actually been around longer than the term 'social protection'. There was the idea of the welfare state, committed to meeting the basic needs of all citizens, socialist states in which these basic needs were all directly provisioned by the state with a significant degree of social equity, and the aspiration in post-colonial countries like ours to bridge the gaps created by centuries of colonial rule by ensuring that all citizens have at least their minimum human needs fulfilled. It is from the aspiration of fulfilling these basic needs for all that some ideas of social protection derive.

There is then a third river of human rights discourse, which begins from the conviction that all persons have some intrinsic human rights, which derive from the shared and equal intrinsic dignity of all human beings. It is the state's duty to ensure that all these human rights are adequately realized, either by directly provisioning them or by creating a regulatory or facilitating regime which ensures the supply of and access to all of these rights.

The Spurious Debate between Bread and Freedom

In the second half of the twentieth century, there was what I regard to be a dubious and sterile debate, but one which held almost all countries across the globe in thrall. The debate was about which sets of rights—social, economic and cultural rights, or civil and political rights—should be guaranteed by the state, and which ones should only be a moral call on the state. In one set of countries—broadly called liberal democracies—civil and political rights are enforceable in independent court systems, but you cannot seek redress from these courts if your social and economic rights are violated. On the other hand, in the socialist world, although the rights discourse was not used, these governments did substantially ensure social and economic rights and extensive social protection. This, however, was at the cost of civil and political freedoms. It was as though people had to choose between bread and freedom. But I believe this was an illegitimate choice because to be human one needs *both* bread and freedom. To me the most exciting and promising discussions on social protection begin from an acceptance of the human rights discourse, of the intrinsic and equal human dignity of all persons, and the indivisibility of all rights—social, economic and cultural rights, as well as civil and political rights. All human beings have a core worth and equal dignity, and for that reason, each deserves the means to live above a floor of human dignity. Indeed at the core of each human right is the affirmation of equal human dignity, therefore each right needs to be upheld to affirm and protect this core equal human dignity of all people. That is the thought-space from which the best discussions around social protections arise.

There is much which is fine in the Constitution of India, but when it was written it was still in some ways located in the dominant understanding of its times; it therefore accepts the prevalent conventional wisdom of the division of rights between those which can be enforced in a court of law, and those which are only moral claims. Accordingly, in our constitution, civil and political rights are listed under the Fundamental Rights, which are legally enforceable. On the other hand, social, economic and cultural rights are subsumed under the Directive Principles, as moral, but not legal claims on the state. But the courts have extended the Fundamental Right to Life to include not just the negative right that the state cannot take away one's life and liberty without due process, as it is conventionally understood in most parts of the world, but also as a *positive* right to life, and that too, a life with dignity. India's Supreme Court held that the fundamental right to life includes also the rights to those which make life with dignity possible—like food, water, health care, education, clean air and shelter. More recently, the executive and the parliament, with legislations like the MGNREGA, the Right of Children to Free and Compulsory Education Act, 2009, and the National Food Security Act, 2013, have taken significant steps towards recognizing the indivisibility of human rights by making these rights—qualified rights to work, education and food—legally enforceable in courts of law. Hopefully in the future, the right to universal healthcare, water and sanitation, the right to shelter and, above all, universal social security will also be enacted.

SOCIAL PROTECTION DISCUSSIONS IN INDIA

These important developments are often not seen to be a part of the social protection discourse in India, though they should be. The discourse in India on social protection has actually been centred on three categories or streams: insurance (life, disability and health insurance), pensions for workers in the unrecognized sector, and a range of unconditional cash transfers. The last comprises modest cash pensions for aged and disabled persons and single women, and for impoverished people officially identified by the state as BPL or 'Below-Poverty-Line'. It was conceptualized by the government in the mid-90s initially for the aged and then gradually expanded. There is also a modest death insurance to protect very poor families in the event of death of the wage-earner. These are all elements of the National Social Assistance Programme, which also included a small maternity benefit provision.

Attempts have been made to expand the coverage and quantum of these kinds of assistance. Only quite recently, social protection discussions have occasionally been reflecting on legally enforceable social and economic rights. Initial drafts of the National Food Security Bill, prepared by the National Advisory Council, included pensions for the aged, disabled and single women as part of the proposed legally enforceable entitlements, but these were eliminated from various official drafts. What is highly significant, however, is that the National Food Security Act passed by the Indian Parliament in 2013 included for the first time a universal provision for maternity benefits, and this is in principle, legally enforceable.

For clarity, in the context of India, I would like to suggest that we first separate the discussion around social security for a) unorganized workers, and b) for people who are outside or 'beyond' work and are excluded from work such as the aged, children in difficult circumstances, women in difficult circumstances including single women, and disabled persons.

Along with unorganized workers who need protection and social security, I think that separately, or complementarily maybe, we need to think of social protection for people who are denied, excluded and pushed out of work, or contrarily are in work when they should not be. Some groups *should* be out of work; children, for instance, should not be in engaged in labor under any circumstances. Social protection is also necessary for children who do not have adult protection, children with single parents who live in the streets, children in conflict areas, children of migrant parents, and so on. Another segment of the population that should be out of *involuntary* work is elderly people. Our studies show us that for most of the impoverished elderly people, there is no retirement age in this country and they have to work to their very last day if they are to eat. Social protection for them would free them from the necessity to work. But on the other end, to the extent that senior people wish to work because their physical and mental condition permits this, and work gives them self-esteem and independence, this right should be recognized and preserved.

Conversely, some people are pushed out or excluded from work—disabled people or single women, for instance—and I think we need to examine these categories. Are they legitimately beyond work because of biological limitations or are they culturally and socially barred from work, as is mostly the case? We must look at their social protection.

Social protection for vulnerable categories 'beyond' work can take two major forms. One is unconditional cash transfers, and the second is non-cash entitlements. In unconditional cash transfers such as pensions and maternity benefits, we need yardsticks to decide an acceptable amount. I suggest that we link it with minimum wages, and something around 10–15 days of minimum wages should be set as the level of unconditional cash transfers for pensions across various vulnerable groups. The coverage should be universal with only the exception of those who are already covered by formal social protection programs.

As for eligibility, we have to use a wider definition of 'singleness', especially for single women, to understand its many categories. Widows right from the age of 18; those who are never married; those who are separated, divorced, abandoned, half widows; and those living in conflict areas and whose husbands have 'disappeared' need to be recognized as vulnerable and therefore be entitled to adequate social protection. We also need a much wider understanding of eligibility under disability and so on.

Maternity benefits in the unorganized sector should also be linked to statutory minimum wages for unorganized workers. They should be treated in the same way as women in the formal sector, who are entitled, typically for six months, to leave on full salaries. The floor of maternity benefits should accordingly be at least six months of statutory minimum wages.

For vulnerable groups, we also need to attend to the mode of dispersal of these cash benefits. We have learnt from our discussions with vulnerable groups who depend on these modest cash transfers for dignified survival that it is clearly important to establish how best these can be accessed every month. There should be transference systems that are within a maximum of two kilometres of where a person lives. The amount should be received on the first day of every month, regardless of budgetary releases. We can use technology such as biometrics, although some say it can and should be done without biometrics. If the state is legally bound to provide these forms of social protection to the most vulnerable person, I think that these are the kinds of questions pertaining to the issue of cash transfers that need to be addressed with respect to this set of people who are 'beyond' work.

Then there is the set of non-cash elements of social protection for this segment of people that I think we need to also talk about. There should be priority selection for all other social programs, such as ration cards or Indira Aawas housing, social housing, etc. The vulnerable groups listed above who are rendered outside work need to be automatically included in every kind of government social provision, being the first in line to be considered for all of these.

Engendering Social Protection in India

Within all of the diverse streams of discussions around social protection in India, there is a need to have a more carefully grounded gendered understanding. Let us first look at the special needs for the social protection of women in the unorganized workforce. There should be universal social security for all workers, both in the formal and informal sectors. This social security should comprise a minimum package of old age and disability pensions, health care, death and disability insurance, and maternity entitlements. Social protection for decent work should be sensitive to the security and special needs of working women. This should not only include factory-based but also home-based and contractual work, domestic work and construction work. We need a deeper understanding of home-based work, (both domestic home-based work and work in home-based industries) and the need for protection around that. Maternity benefits and crèches at workplaces are largely neglected. There should be sensitivity within the design of social protection programs to cater to women's work, including single women and older women.

Also, if you are looking from a gendered perspective, in India's

National Maternity Benefits Scheme, at least when it was initially drafted and enforced, there was a provision for unconditional cash transfer—a very modest amount but for all BPL women who were expecting and nursing. But, the central government, along the way, decided that even maternity benefits needed to be made conditional, to create incentives for women to have smaller families, to get vaccinated and choose to deliver in institutions. So the conditionality that was associated with the maternity scheme came in. Our big problem with conditionalities is that, in a sense, they penalize the intended beneficiary by making maternity benefits, in this case, contingent on these many conditions. Does a woman have the power to make decisions about her reproduction? There may be no institutions where she can go or she may be too poor for the opportunity costs. So the importance of unconditional maternity benefits needs to be in our priorities. The National Food Security Act, 2013, does not entail any conditionality for the universal maternity benefits it mandates, but there is still a danger that this may be introduced as the central and state governments actually roll out these entitlements.

There is also the limited understanding of what constitutes 'singleness' for pensions. Pensions today are mostly restricted to older widows, but do not recognize the problems of younger widows, divorced, separated, abandoned and never-married women.

Another gendered problem is that many food transfer programs such as take-home rations for pregnant women, neglect intra-family inequalities. She is given five or 10 kilos of uncooked food grains, with the facile expectation that this will go into her stomach. This neglects family inequities of power and access because of which all of this take-home ration is most likely to enter the common pot of the family, of which only a small fraction will come to the woman. Another problem is that most programs for food transfers for pregnant women are justified as being necessary for the health of the child in her womb. This instrumentalizes women as reproducers rather than valuing them intrinsically in and for themselves. It is as if she has no right to nutrition in her own capacity, independent of any instrumentality as a mother.

Let me illustrate some of the non-cash entitlements for social protection I would recommend for one social category: widows and single women.

- In addition to priority selection for all relevant government referred to earlier, their children should have priority selection in all government residential schools, and priority in land allotments.
- Single women and their dependent minor children should be recognized as separate households for purposes of ration cards and other entitlements, even while living as part of a larger joint household.
- Single mothers should be able to avail special crèches and child care services.
- Single working women's hostels need to be expanded.
- For women who have suffered violence, comprehensive social services need to be put in place.
- Protection for children of single women should be ensured by making them automatically eligible for admission in state-run or government hostels, or social welfare hostels.

Conclusion: Rights and Caring

To summarize, in India we have witnessed several diverse discussions around social protection, and the actual extension of these protections has been halting for the most part. We need firstly to commit ourselves to the social contract which Chomsky spoke of, of our obligation in a good society to take care of each other. This entails that we recognize and address the needs of unorganized workers, including women as unorganized workers and their comprehensive needs of social protection recognized as universal rights. We need to look at women and people 'beyond' work, children in care of need and protection, old people, infirm people, persons with disabilities, and single people, and consider again their comprehensive and universal rights-based social protection, including both unconditional cash transfers as well as non-cash elements of social protection.

To operationalize all of these obligations, we need to construct a legal scaffolding of universal social and economic rights, including rights to food, education, health-care, shelter, maternity benefits and social protection. It is only with such a universal human rights framework that we can become a society in which we actually care for each other, and only then can we will build an India which truly, actively cares for all, and which recognizes the intrinsic equal dignity of all persons, regardless of gender, caste, class, faith and disability.

References

Chomsky, Noam (2011), 'The state-corporate complex: A threat to freedom and survival', text of lecture given at the The University of Toronto. Available at: http://www.chomsky.info/talks/20110407.htm

Holzman, R., Sherburne-Benz, L. and Tesliuc, E. (2003) 'Social risk management: The World Bank's approach to social protection in a globalizing world', Washington D.C.: World Bank.

UN (1966), 'International covenant on civil and political rights' Available at: http://www.ohchr.org/en/professionalinterest/pages/ccpr.aspx

UN (1966), 'International covenant on economic, social and cultural rights' Available at: http://www.ohchr.org/Documents/ProfessionalInterest/cescr.pdf

Unpacking Social Protection from a Women's Rights Lens

SEJAL DAND

The artificial dichotomy of civil-political rights and socio-economic rights collapses when viewed from the lens of a woman from a land-owning family in Uttar Pradesh, who is beaten by her husband when she steps out to work for wages instead of working on her family farm. In the violation of her right to security and mobility, civil and political rights combine seamlessly with the violation of her economic and social rights. The persistence of different forms of gender based violence affect women disproportionately. The underlying structural causes of the widespread prevalence of different forms of violence against women across all societies lie in the persistence of gender discrimination and inequalities, causing deprivation and producing vulnerability. Bodily integrity[1] and decision making are important factors for determining women's labor outcomes and are intrinsically linked to individual women's civil and political rights. These, along with other measures of access

---

[1] Martha Nussbaum in her capabilities defines bodily integrity as, 'Being able to move freely from place to place; to be secure against violent assault, including sexual assault and domestic violence; having opportunities for sexual satisfaction and for choice in matters of reproduction.'

and control over resources, have an impact on their realization of economic-social rights. Hence, from the women's rights perspective, bodily integrity becomes critical to the framing of social protection.

Social protection floors can be used as tools to 'prevent and reduce poverty, inequality, social exclusion and social insecurity, and promote equal opportunity and gender equality'[2] only when they are designed to transform gender roles and when they address the unequal social relations of power stemming from intersectionalities, and comprehensively take measures to address gender-based violence.

Recognizing Multiple Forms of Women's Work

The lack of recognition of women's work is not limited to women's unpaid work in households, family-owned enterprises, farms, etc. It extends to all unpaid care work, including domestic work (meal preparation, cleaning, washing clothes, water and fuel collection) and direct care of persons (including children, older persons and persons with disabilities, but also able-bodied adults) undertaken in homes and communities. It deems women's labor during reproduction, breastfeeding and nurturing as natural duties. This is now extended to encompass a large part of public and community work. A huge number of women employed in public programs such as ICDS, MDMS and healthcare lack the rights of workers, including decent wages, safe work conditions and social protection. Increasingly, most government programs are now relying on women's groups for ensuring community mobilization, awareness, and participation and monitoring, without compensating for their time, labor or skills.

---

[2] Recommendation on National Floors for Social Protection (No. 202) adopted in the 101st session in the International Labour Conference.

Gaps in Program Implementation Arising from Policy Frameworks

The lack of conceptual clarity on gender equality in social protection permeates down to the program design and implementation mechanisms of social protection schemes. This results in gender-blind formulations of program objectives as well as the creation of access barriers to social protection for the most vulnerable women. One such example is maternity entitlements in India, which are perhaps the most significant entitlements for women to be universalized under the National Food Security Act (NFSA, 2013), and which come with the caveat: 'subject to the schemes framed by the central government'. Therefore, the policy framework and design of the schemes of the central government, which are currently operational become important for the realization of this intervention of social security.

The failure of the Maternity Entitlements Act (1961) in reaching most women led to the launch of the National Maternity Benefit Scheme (NMBS) in 2001, which provided for a sum of Rs. 500 per pregnancy for women belonging to poor households, for pre-natal and post-natal maternity care up to a woman's first two live births. This scheme was targeted at women of 19 years of age and above. It was followed by another pilot scheme, launched in 52 districts across the country in 2010, called the Indira Gandhi Matritva Sahyog Yojana[3] (IGMSY), which offered conditional maternity benefits.[4]

---

[3] Indira Gandhi Matritva Sahyog Yojana (IGMSY) is a flagship program of the government of India under the Ministry of Women and Child Development that targets pregnant and lactating women 19 years of age and older for their first two live births. Indira Gandhi Matritva Sahyog Yojana (IGMSY), introduced in 2010, is a Conditional Cash Transfer scheme for pregnant and lactating (P&L) women.

[4] http://wcd.nic.in/schemes/igmsyscheme.pdf (accessed on 29 July 2013).

In its introduction to the policy framework, IGMSY quotes the Eleventh Five-Year Plan document:

> Poor women continue to work to earn a living for the family right up to the last days of their pregnancy, thus not being able to put on as much weight as they otherwise might. They also resume working soon after childbirth, even though their bodies might not permit it—preventing their bodies from fully recovering, and their ability to exclusively breastfeed their new born in the first six months. Therefore, there is urgent need for introducing a modest maternity benefit to partly compensate for their wage loss.

However, when the scheme is launched the program objectives lose focus on the maternity rights of women and instrumentalize the partial wage compensation as a cash incentive to promote 'appropriate practices, care and service utilization during pregnancy, safe delivery and lactation'. The conditionalities imposed in the scheme not only ignore the current supply-side gaps in health and nutrition public services, but also penalize the most vulnerable women through targeting. The scheme denies maternity benefits to women who are below 19 years of age on the grounds of encouraging marriage and child birth at the right age. It restricts maternity benefits up to two live births with an ostensible concern for women's health, ignoring the widespread gender discrimination prevalent in society where most women in this country have no control over decisions regarding their marriage or fertility. The restriction of maternity entitlements for women who are 19 years or above, and have up to two children has to be seen in a context where the median age at marriage among women age 25–49 is only 16.8 years, as per the National Family Health Survey (2005–6), and young women of age 15–19 account for almost one-fifth of total fertility. Not only are these the very women and children who have high mortality risks, along with women who have multiparous pregnancies and who consist of those belonging to schedule caste and tribes and who have been denied education. The conditionalities in the program design itself practically exclude the ones who need the protection, leave alone putting in mechanisms that proactively reach out to the most vulnerable or make the executive accountable for the exclusions.

Ensuring Women's Independent Rights to Social Protection

Many social practices, traditions and religious beliefs relegate women to a secondary status within the household and sometimes even the state denies adult women their status as legal majors, subsuming them under the household, wherein she can never be considered the head of household if she is married or there is an adult male in the same household. An example from the national social assistance program is of the National Family Benefit Scheme, which provides for one time assistance of Rs. 20,000 in the event of the death of 'the primary breadwinner'. Though not stated anywhere, in practice this has been interpreted by the executive to mean a male member, whereas, in reality, in a poor family all adult members contribute to the family's livelihood and more so do women.

Social security measures are often targeted at families/households without taking into account the intra-household gender inequalities. For example, in India households identified as living below poverty line are supposed to get entitlements related to housing, health cover, food. However, the state has no mechanism to ensure that the entitlements are distributed equally within the household or that women have equal access and control over these resources. As a result, these entitlements have little impact on the well-being of women or on building their capabilities. Wherever women have had independent rights, they have been able to struggle to assert these rights and engage the state on those issues. Several studies of the Mahatma Gandhi National Rural Employment Scheme (MNREGS)[5] show that women's collection and control over wages is high, enabling them to negotiate within the household, wherever wages are paid to them directly or transferred to their accounts. Even in the Indira Gandhi National Old Age Pensions Scheme (IGNOAPS),[6] the number of women availing of their pensions equals the number of men since there is no dependence on the executive to or mediated by the consent of the spouse who is considered the head of the household.

Women in India face multiple challenges in realizing their entitlements since they have almost no records except voting cards in their own names. Few have a house or land in their names, birth certificates or electricity/telephone/mobile bills or independent bank accounts, which are commonly used to establish domicile. This compounds the operational difficulties in asserting or demanding entitlements. Hence, it is imperative on the state to recognize women as independent entities and ensure portability of their rights.

Social Protection as a Universal Right: Excluding No One and Recognizing Multiple Vulnerabilities

The substantive model of equality is concerned with equal opportunity, but even more so, with equality of results. It

---

[5] The Mahatma Gandhi National Rural Employment Guarantee Act aims at enhancing the livelihood security of people in rural areas by guaranteeing hundred days of wage-employment in a financial year to a rural household whose adult members volunteer to do unskilled manual work.

[6] The government of India has provided for the National Old Age Pension Scheme as one of the sub-schemes of the National Social Assistance Program. It came into existence with effect from 15 August 1995, with the aim to provide social assistance to poor people in households, who are above 60 years of age, as old-age pension.

stresses equal treatment as well as equal access and equal benefits. It recognizes that women and men may have to be treated differently in order for them to benefit equally. Feminists from the global south have long recognized that social relations of caste, class, ethnicity, sexuality are integral to defining gender equalities. These have to be taken into account when providing enabling conditions and/or affirmative action.

Currently, social protection measures do not account for these multiple vulnerabilities. Rather, the discourse focuses on uniform social assistance because we talk of universalization. However, a sex worker may be vulnerable to state violence because her work itself is not recognized. A woman whose husband deserts her and is now single, will not be entitled to a widow's pension, though she is equally vulnerable. A disabled old woman requires greater assistance, but is only allowed to draw on one social assistance scheme. These multiple dimensions of vulnerabilities need to be addressed specifically.

We are talking of the right to social protection as a universal right, but from on-the-ground experience we know that there are still exclusions. The homeless woman, the child migrant laborer, the sex worker, the tribal woman, the woman whose husband has been labeled a terrorist and is reportedly missing, will get excluded by design or default. We have to recognize the specific vulnerabilities of each of these groups, deconstruct the mechanisms of exclusion to ensure that the universal right to social protection accords primacy to the principle of automatic inclusion of those who are most vulnerable to exclusion.

Investing in Organizing and Mobilizing Women and Women's Institutions

The full range of social protection interventions comprises protective, preventive, promotive and transformative measures (Devereux and Sabates-Wheeler, 2006). Social protection interventions which have transformative potential seek to address concerns of social equity and exclusion through social empowerment (e.g., collective action for workers' rights, building voice and authority in decision-making for women).

The state has failed to address gender discrimination substantially and protect women's right to equality. For instance, inheritance laws in the country that recognize women's equal rights to land ownership have been prevalent for over 50 years, yet they have never been implemented on the ground, resulting in only 11% of women land owners in India, of which a substantial number is that of women-headed households/widows.

Evidence from across India, of organizing women through the formation of groups, unions, federations, community based organizations shows that these enhance the voice and agency of women to engage with institutions of community/state, which, in turn, affects the ability of women to negotiate social relations within the household.

This material investment and support for women's organizations have to be an integral part of the social protection floor. Otherwise, it will be impossible to challenge the underlying patriarchies embedded in the institutions of family, community, state and market.

Reference

Devereux, Stephen and Sabates-Wheeler, Rachel (2006), 'Transformative social protection', Brighton: Institute of Development Studies.

The Human Right to Social Protection and the Post-2015 Development Agenda

Human rights, inclusive development and reduction of inequalities through income guarantees and care for all

Dr. Timo Voipio

Summary

This article makes four points, on rights—inequalities, inclusion, and care.

Rights: While the Indian reader will know the many remaining challenges of the Indian social protection systems, it is also important to recognize its achievements: India has recently become a source of inspiration for the rest of the world interested in providing rights-based social protection guarantees to all children, women and men—poor and well-off alike. The legal guarantees of the MGNREGA[1] and other Indian social

---

[1] MGNREGA: Mahatma Gandhi National Rural Employment Guarantee Act. See: http://nrega.nic.in

protection and employment guarantee schemes are real-life examples of what the UN Social Protection Floor Initiative aims at. Implementation challenges obviously remain and must be addressed.

Inequalities: The reduction of inequalities of all kinds must become the central objective of everything we do. The global commitment to poverty reduction is morally admirable but operationally ineffective, as long as we measure progress only in terms of rising averages, without recognizing rising inequalities and the stagnation in the rights and livelihoods of the poorest. By promoting laws, policies and programs aimed at reducing gender inequality and socio-economic inequalities we are going to succeed in poverty reduction, too, but not the other way round.

Inclusion: All our economic and social policies need to be inclusive. They have to recognize the human rights of every woman, man, child and older person as an individual rights-holder, not as a 'dependent' of her husband, father or some other 'primary' household member. An important litmus test for the inclusiveness of national as well as global policies is whether or not they include explicit language about the rights of persons—women and men—with disabilities (10–15% of each population) and whether they genuinely promote meaningful participation of all women and men—'all' meaning really all, including those with disabilities or other handicaps. The global MDG-agenda failed on this account. So, we need to do better with the post-2015 global development agenda.

Care: Finally, the value of care work—performed mostly by women—has to be recognized, professionals of care to be empowered, and the role of ministries and departments of community development, women, children and social affairs should be recognized, respected and boosted.

India as a Source of Inspiration

India is today a source of inspiration for the rest of the world, interested in providing rights-based social protection guarantees to all children, women and men—poor and less poor alike. The Mahatma Gandhi National Rural Employment Guarantee Scheme (MGNREGA), the national health insurance scheme, Rashtriya Swasthya Bima Yojana (RSBY), and a number of other social protection programs designed and implemented by both the federal and state governments of India, and by civil society organizations have become famous models of 'good practice' that governments of many other countries are trying to learn from and emulate or adapt to their different contexts.

Today social protection is widely considered an important pillar of global development efforts, including the Post-2015 Agenda. It is hard to believe that even in the year 2000, when the United Nations Millennium Declaration was discussed and the Millennium Development Goals (MDGs) launched, no one felt that social protection was worth mentioning even once.

Since then, Indian and other South Asian employment guarantee schemes as well as the child grant and social pension schemes of both Brazil and South Africa, the health insurance of Thailand, Rwanda and Ghana, and the 'productive safety net' of Ethiopia—among several others—have become inspirational examples and influential models of a rights-based commitment by an increasing number of governments to ensure that no child, woman or man has to fall below a 'Social Protection Floor'—a nationally specified level of minimum income and basic service protection necessary for human dignity.

This same spirit of leaving no one behind was included, as the first recommendation, in the report of the UN High-Level Panel on the Post-2015 Development Agenda.

Human Rights-based Approach to Social Protection

This is all still work in progress. Under the international human rights law, each child, woman and man has the right not to be left behind. The right to social security and adequate or decent standard of living is guaranteed to each individual as per the United Nations' Universal Declaration of Human Rights (UDHR, esp. Art. 22 & 25) and the International Covenant on Economic, Social and Cultural Rights (ICESCR, esp. Art. 7 & 9).[2]

The right to social security represents an important legal guarantee aimed at ensuring the right of everyone to live a life with dignity, and to maintain a dignified livelihood. Implementation of this right is an essential precondition for the realization of other human rights. The recognition of social security as a human right represents an essential transformation from needs-based charity to rights-based social justice (Darooka, 2008).

---

[2] The two concepts, social security and social protection, have different meanings in different countries and languages, subject to the historical evolution of social policies. In the United States, the term social security refers to a specific social insurance program for the retired and the disabled. Elsewhere, the term is used in a much broader sense, referring to the economic security society offers when people are faced with certain life-cycle related risks of impoverishment. In some countries the term social security refers mainly to contributory social insurance schemes related to formal employment contracts, while social protection has a broader connotation, including also non-contributory (tax-funded) social assistance, essential social services and labor market measures. In India as well as in my own country, Finland, the concept social security is more commonly used and understood as an *outcome*, that social protection is a *means* for. The UN Universal Declaration of Human Rights (Art. 22) and the International Covenant on Economic, Social and Cultural Rights (ICESCR, Art. 9) speak of social security, but currently the ILO, which is the leading global normative authority on social security/ social protection, uses the terms social protection and social security pretty much inter-changeably. See: http://www.ilo.org/secsoc/areas-of-work/legal-advice/WCMS_205341/lang--en/index.htm

States are legally obligated to establish social protection systems that provide a guaranteed minimum level of social security in all lifecycle situations for each resident, and progressively higher levels of protection to as many as possible.

Not only the progressively improving final *outcomes* of social protection programs, but also the *process* through which such programs are designed, implemented and evaluated, must respect the human rights principles. Core among them are universality, equality and non-discrimination, accessibility, acceptability, adequacy and the incorporation of the gender perspective, meaningful participation, transparency and accountability (Sepúlveda and Nyst, 2012).

The essential principle of *universality* means that every child, woman and man has an equal *individual right* to at least basic social protection against the risks of impoverishment in *lifecycle situations* such as sickness, disability, maternity, employment injury, unemployment, old age, death of a family member, high health care or child care costs, and general poverty and social exclusion.

Social protection measures can include, for instance, cash transfer schemes, social care services, unemployment or disability benefits, public work and employment guarantee programs, minimum wage legislation, school stipends and lunches, social pensions, food vouchers and transfers, user fee exemptions for health care or education, and subsidized essential services.[3]

---

[3] Or, to use a broader definition of Darooka (2008), social security implies overall security for a person within the family, work place, and society in general. It includes measures designed to ensure that all citizens receive certain basic standards of personal security which consist of: their basic needs (such as adequate nutrition, shelter, education, health care, clean water and food supplies) protection from contingencies (such as illness, disability, accidents, death, unemployment, medical care, child birth, child care, widowhood, and old age), protection against natural disasters, and an environment free from violence (including sexual harassment and domestic violence).

The principles of equality and non-discrimination require, for example, that states eliminate discrimination in law, policy and practice, and take special measures to *protect the most vulnerable* members of society *as a matter of priority*. This means that social protection programs must be available to all those who suffer from structural or cultural discrimination such as women, children, older persons, persons with disabilities, ethnic minorities, indigenous peoples, people with HIV/AIDS, and other marginalized and excluded people.

Impact of Social Protection on Gender Inequality

Considering that gender inequality is a cause of and a factor that perpetuates poverty, effective social protection strategies must be designed to promote *gender equality,* protect *women's rights* and *empower women*. In order to do so, many social protection schemes have decided to transfer cash only to women, as it is widely understood that women typically spend the cash benefits for purposes that improve the education, health and nutritional levels of children.

The experience of conditional cash transfer programs in Brazil, Honduras, Mexico, Nicaragua and South Africa has, indeed, shown that children, particularly girls, in households with female pension recipients are more likely to be healthier and to attend school than if a male receives the grant (Samson et al., 2006).

However, the impact of social protection systems is not gender neutral, and channeling social protection to women does not ensure that the root causes of gender inequality will be adequately addressed (Jones et al., 2008). From discriminatory legal frameworks to persistent discriminatory social norms, there are many underlying causes that may prevent women from benefiting from social protection, or accessing social services in an equal manner to men.

States must therefore ensure that programs are designed, implemented and monitored taking into account the different experiences of men and women. To ensure that men and women benefit equally, social protection systems must address *women's life-cycle risks* and the *burden of care* (for children and the elderly) that they bear, as well as the differences in *access* to services, work and productive activities between women and men.

For example, when women are made responsible for complying with *conditions* (or *co-responsibilities*) or when they are required to *travel* (sometimes long distances) to collect social protection benefits or to participate in the management or monitoring of social protection programs, their *unpaid workload* increases. The additional demands on their time may hinder women and girls from accessing formal labor markets, limit their possibilities to participate in capacity building including education and training, or deprive them of leisure time. A program that increases the time a mother spends away from home may also have a detrimental effect on girls' schooling, if girls are then required to assume the mother's activities such as cooking or collecting water (Thakur et al., 2009; Davies, 2009).

Some social protection programs have innovated flexible gender-sensitive arrangements to avoid such negative unintended consequences and to tap into complementary benefits. The Indian MGNREGA and the Ethiopian Productive Safety Net Programme (PSNP) both guarantee availability of income earning opportunities within walking distance from the homes of beneficiaries, which makes it easier and safer for women to join (Andrews and Kryeziu, 2013). Both also include provisions for child care facilities.

According to the guidelines of the Ethiopian PSNP, the work requirement should be waived for older or pregnant women. The local public work project managers of PSNP are also expected to actively innovate projects with outputs that reduce women's work burden, such as fuelwood, lots or water points, and working on private land owned by female-headed households, but these guidelines have generally not been implemented (World Bank, 2010). However, many women feel that participating in public works improved their standing and respect in the community. Some report that men took on more domestic work. With PSNP providing income-earning opportunities in the home village, teenage girls and young women had less need to move to towns to work as domestic employees, where they are often subjected to abuse (Combaz, 2013).

Realizing the Right to Social Protection for All, in All Countries

Despite these promising examples, very few countries have, till date, succeeded in protecting all residents against all life-cycle poverty risks. But a dynamic and interesting process of practical, mutual learning is under way across continents, as nations are gradually extending their systems of social protection, both in terms of people and risks covered.

At the same time, wide global coalitions of international agencies, governments and social partners are today united in advocating inter-governmental normative resolutions that put the idea of social protection floors right at the center of the global Post-2015 agenda of rights-based, inclusive, inequality-reducing and sustainable development. The ILO Recommendation 202 (2012) on nationally defined social protection floors was an important opening—now there is an 'agreed language' from an inter-governmental forum that can be easily copy-pasted to more inter-governmental resolutions in other UN forums.

This ILO Recommendation 202 was unanimously[4] approved by all governments, employer federations and trade unions of the world. It provides four nationally defined guarantees of 1) health and maternity care services; 2) income security for all

---

[4] With only one abstention among 142 governments.

children and for families caring for children; 3) income security for the unemployed and those persons with disabilities (PWD) who are able to work; 4) pensions for those older persons and PWD who are not able to work.

'Nationally defined' means that there is no global one-size-fits-all formula as to how the basic human right to social protection is to be achieved and at what levels. Some countries will want to use contributory social insurance, some tax-funded social assistance, and in many countries there are going to be hybrid combinations of these approaches.

Global political support for the idea of government-funded minimum social protection crystallized in 2009, when the heads of the United Nations agencies launched the One-UN Social Protection Floor Initiative. Finland has been one of the active sponsors of this UN initiative from the very beginning.

Partnerships for Rights and Equality

I have come to know the Indian Programme on Women's Economic, Social and Cultural Rights (PWESCR) as one of the most skillful and effective advocates of the right to social security protection for all.

My government (of Finland) shares this commitment to a Human Rights Based Approach (HRBA) to development, which includes civil and political rights and freedom as well as economic, social and cultural rights. Finland gives special emphasis to the rights of women, children, ethnic minorities and indigenous peoples, the rights of persons with disabilities, those living with HIV/AIDS, and the rights of sexual and gender minorities.

In Finland's Development Policy Programme extreme poverty is identified as the world's greatest human rights issue. It starts, in line with the UN Universal Declaration of Human Rights, from the idea that all human beings are born free and equal in status and rights. The goal of human rights based development work is a situation in which the poorest women and men, as *rights-holders*, know their rights and are able to advocate for them. It is equally important that the authorities, as duty-bearers, know their human-rights obligations and have the capacity to promote these rights.

To be human rights based, development policy should promote the core human rights principles such as universality, self-determination, non-discrimination and equality.

We know from Finland's own experience, that inequality and exclusion prevent development. Finland was a poor country torn by a bloody civil war and living on subsistence agriculture and forestry till just one hundred years ago. Now Finland comes close to the top in many global rankings of genuine progress, competitiveness, students' learning outcomes, and ranks last on the global ranking of Least Failed States.[5]

Gender equality has always been an essential element in Finland's transformative social and economic policies, goal-consciously striving towards a 'Society for All', inclusive of all women and men, girls and boys. Besides human rights and social justice reasons there have been strong economic motivations for Finland's inclusive and equality-oriented policies. Inequalities create social conflicts which lead to a waste of economic opportunities. A sense of social justice in turn creates social cohesion and vast amounts of economically valuable social capital. Social mobility is another economic good. To be economically successful, a nation cannot afford not to unlock and 'tap into' all of its talents and human resources. This requires equal and universal socio-economic policies that create equal opportunities for all women and men to participate in, contribute to and benefit from productive and reproductive economic activities (OECD-POVNET, 2006).

---

[5] http://ffp.statesindex.org/rankings-2013-sortable

The Finnish experience shows also that policies other than those specifically targeting gender equality have often had an important positive influence on gender equality (Wiman, 2010). Despite the turbulent history and poverty of the nation, Finland introduced some of these key social protection and social service policies at a time when the country was still a poor, agricultural, developing country: free primary education for all (1921), universal social pension for all (1937), statutory school meals for all pupils (1943), universal health insurance (1963), and free secondary education for all (1970s).

Some of the key gender specific institutional social protection innovations have been equality of inheritance rights of women and men (1878), maternity allowance and 'maternity package'(essential clothes and child care utensils, 1937), maternity and child welfare clinics (1944), universal child care allowance (1948), universal maternity leave (1949), municipal child care (1973), paternity leave (1978), etc.

Inclusive and Inequality Reducing Development

MDGs have constituted the core consensus of international development efforts since the year 2000. The MDG-target year is 2015 and therefore, the governments of the world are now not only busy trying to reach the MDGs but are also already debating the key elements of a new post-2015 global development framework in the UN.

The key issues that the MDGs failed us on are human rights, inclusion, inequality reduction, social protection and disability. Still in 1995, at the Copenhagen Social Summit, we had committed ourselves to the 'promotion and protection of all human rights, non-discrimination, inclusion and participation of all people (including disadvantaged and vulnerable persons), as well as to the reduction of inequalities (by removing any political, legal, economic and social factors that foster inequality).'

One of the key goals we had agreed on in Copenhagen in 1995 was that 'all people should have adequate economic and social protection during unemployment, ill health, maternity, child rearing, widowhood, disability and old age.' We didn't call it the Social Protection Floor at that time but the idea was the same.

Under the heading of 'Inclusive Development' the Copenhagen Declaration spoke about persons with disabilities: 'One of the world's largest minorities, more than 1 in 10, are people with disabilities (PWD), who are too often forced into poverty, unemployment and social isolation.' In Copenhagen all governments of the world committed themselves to 'ensuring that persons with disabilities are included…and that society… responds to the rights of PWDs…by making the physical and social environment accessible.'

But then, very strangely, in the year 2000 the MDGs had nothing to say about the right to social protection. They also ignored PWDs completely. The intensified efforts of the global community of PWDs and disabled people's organizations (DPOs) then led to the signing of the UN Convention on the Human Rights of Persons with Disabilities (CRPD) in 2006.

We could—and should—use the case of PWDs as a litmus test of the inclusiveness of our policies. If our policies and actions are inclusive and accessible for persons with disabilities, we can trust them as most likely to be inclusive of *all* people.

We Can Do Better—Social Protection Floor is an Effective Approach

The new Post-2015 Development Agenda is a great opportunity for us to do better in the years to come. Something has gone terribly wrong during the years we have been implementing the MDG-Agenda; inequalities have grown dramatically in nearly all societies, and globally.

We have failed to empower the poorest and the most disadvantaged and socially excluded people. In the post-2015 era we have to stop monitoring averages and focus our attention specifically on the changes in the lives of the bottom quintile and other disadvantaged and excluded groups.

But take note, I am not speaking in favor of narrow poverty targeting; programs targeted only on the poor tend to become poor programs over time. In many cases the rights and interests of the poorest children, women and men can be most effectively promoted by developing nation-wide universal social and economic policies and programs that bring benefits to—and gain the political support of—all residents, especially the politically influential middle classes. Inequality-reducing cross-subsidization is easy to build into such programs, and their effectiveness in supporting positive changes, particularly in the lives of the poorest and most disadvantaged population groups, can be reliably monitored.

Social Protection is Good for the Economy

So, there are good human rights arguments in support of social protection. But there are also strong economic arguments. I chaired the Social Protection Task Team of the Poverty Network of the OECD (Organisation of Economic Cooperation and Development), i.e., OECD-POVNET. Our mission was to convince the chief economists of our ministries of finance and the international financial institutions that investments into social protection should not be regarded as cost items in the national accounts. Instead, they should be conceived as high-return investments that help unlock the optimal productive potential of the most important productive factor of every economy, the women and men.

We summarized the Pro-Poor Growth arguments of social protection by saying that social protection (a) can empower poor women and men to participate in, contribute to and benefit from growth; (b) can promote innovation, risk taking and entrepreneurship; (c) can counteract irreversible asset depletion in desperate survival situations; (d) broadens the tax base and enhances the aggregate demand, both of which are good for the economy; (e) and supports social mobility, which is a way to ensure that all the potential talents of the nation can be unlocked to support national development.

Encouraging Opportunities in Socially Protective 'Multi-Purpose' Programs

Besides care and income protection, the best social protection programs can provide many other benefits. For instance, employment guarantee schemes—like the Indian NREGA—could be used not only to protect income and food security but also for skills training for large numbers of rural women and men who have not been able to access formal vocational training institutions.

Public works programs often focus on building necessary community infrastructure, such as feeder roads, class rooms, health clinics, water and sanitation structures, rainwater harvesting systems, etc. With intensified training inputs these programs can transfer valuable—and even marketable—work skills to young women and men, and if a skill certification system can be integrated into the program, the young women and men can even get an officially recognized certificate of the skills they have acquired.

Socially protective public works can also be focused on natural resource, forestry and watershed-management tasks. In these cases social protection/public works programs can make an important contribution to vocational skills training and learning in the field of 'green jobs'.

Recognize the Critically Important Role of Social Care Work, Care Workers, and the Ministries Responsible for Care Work

Several developing countries have already shown that with clear political will, it is possible to design and build nationwide programs that create a solid Social Protection Floor (SPF) for everyone. Social protection is an effective way to reduce inequalities and to promote everyone's human right to meaningful participation in society and economy.

Also, over the past three to four years, nearly all of the leading international agencies—including ILO, WFP, FAO, UNICEF, UN Women and the World Bank—have drafted, often through wide consultations, new long-term strategies for social protection. The UN agencies launched a joint One-UN Social Protection Floor Initiative in 2009, supported, among others, by my government. The G20 Development Group saw the benefits of coordination and cooperation between the leading agencies, and gave a mandate to institutionalize this coordination work in the form of a Social Protection Inter-Agency Cooperation Board or SPIAC-B.

So there is now a historically strong international support for social protection as a key priority of international development efforts.

Yet, social protection requires much more than just cash transfers. An emerging lesson from global experience is that cash transfers alone are not as effective as cash plus key complementary interventions. Gender-related examples include providing childcare support for working mothers, enhancing recipients' access to the labor market through job training, and linking to agricultural input support. This kind of integrated approach responds to the importance of recognizing women's needs as workers as well as their needs as mothers.

It is essential to recognize the value and role of the care work, i.e. reproductive work that women typically provide informally within families and communities. Cash alone will never be able to transform the lives of disadvantaged children, women and men. And social protection systems will never succeed without the critically important contributions of professionally competent and motivated professionals of care, i.e., social workers.

One of the best ways to empower women and to enable women to move forward in their working careers is to formalize and professionalize care work. Professional care work can provide lots of formal sector employment opportunities, with individual social and health insurance benefits to women as well as men. And the high quality child, health and elderly care services—funded through general tax revenues—can give peace of mind to and liberate a great number of professionally trained women to take an active role in the professional labor markets, providing a major boost of creativity, skills and intellect to the business and government circles of the nation.

The ministries responsible for social transfers and care—ministries of social affairs, community development and children's and women's affairs—are often among the financially weakest ministries in most developing countries. This is a major difference compared to Finland, where the Ministry of Social Affairs and Health is the ministry with the largest budget. The treasury of my country does not regard social protection as a cost, but as a reproductive investment into the most valuable productive factor of our national economy, its people.

References

Andrews, Colin and Kryeziu, Adea (2013), 'Public works and the jobs agenda: Pathways for social cohesion', Background paper for the World Development Report, World Bank. Available at: http://siteresources.worldbank.org/EXTNWDR2013/Resources/8258024-1320950747192/8260293-1320956712276/8261091-1348683883703/WDR2013_bp_Social_Cohesion_and_Public_ orks.pdf

Combaz, Emilie (2013), 'Social inclusion in productive safety net programmes', GSDRC Helpdesk Research Report 1005, Birmingham, UK: GSDRC, University of Birmingham. Available at: http://www.gsdrc.org/docs/open/HDQ1005.pdf

Darooka, Priti (2008), 'Social security: A woman's human right', PWESCR Discussion paper No. 2. New Delhi: Programme for Women's Economic, Social and Cultural Rights (PWESCR). Available at: http://www.pwescr.org/Social_Sercuity_Paper.pdf

Jones, Nicola, Holmes Rebecca, and Espey Jessica (2008), 'Gender and the MDGs briefing paper no. 42', London: Overseas Development Institute, London. Available at: http://www.odi.org.uk/sites/odi.org.uk/files/odi-assets/publications-opinion-files/3270.pdf

Kabeer, Naila (2008), *Mainstreaming Gender in Social Protection for the Informal Economy*, London: Commonwealth Secretariat. Available at: http://publications.thecommonwealth.org/mainstreaming-gender-in-social-protection-for-the-informal-economy-429-p.aspx

Mehta, Anupma and Ahluwalia, Meenakshi (2013), *Women's Social Security and Protection in India*, A report from a National Conference 6–7 May 2013, New Delhi: PWESCR. Available at: http://www.pwescr.org/PWESCR_Report%20for%20Web_23-11-2013.pdf

OECD-POVNET (2006), *Promoting Pro-Poor Growth: Key policy messages*, Paris: Poverty Network (POVNET) of the OECD Development Assistance Committee (DAC). Available at: http://www.oecd.org/dac/povertyreduction/promotingpro-poorgrowthkeypolicymessagesand2006policystatement.htm

——— (2009), *Promoting Pro-Poor Growth: Social Protection*, Paris: Poverty Network (POVNET) of the OECD Development Assistance Committee (DAC). Available at: http://www.oecd.org/dac/povertyreduction/promotingpro-poorgrowthsocialprotection.htm

Samson, Michael, van Niekerk, Irene and MacQuene, Kenneth (2006), *Designing and Implementing Social Transfer Programmes*, Cape town: Economic Policy Research Institute (EPRI). Available at: http://www.unicef.org/socialpolicy/files/designing_and_implementing_social_transfer_programmes.pdf

Thakur, Sarojini Ganju, Arnold, Catherine and Johnson, Tina (2009), *Gender and Social Protection*, Paris: OECD-POVNET. Available at: http://www.oecd.org/dataoecd/26/34/43280899.pdf

Uppsala (2013), *The Uppsala Statement by Global Civil Society Organisations on the Right to Social Security*, Church of Sweden. Available at: http://www.lotcobistand.org/pdf/Uppsala_Statement.pdf

Wiman, Ronald (2010), *Mainstreaming the Gender Perspective into Social Development*, Paper contributed to the International Conference on Promoting Empowerment of Women in Arab Countries, 5–6 October 2010, Tunis. Available at: http://www.thl.fi/en_US/web/en/topics/information_packages/gsp/reduction/gender_equality

World Bank (2010), *Designing and Implementing a Rural Safety Net in a Low Income Setting: Lessons learned from Ethiopia's Productive Safety Net Program 2005–2009*, World Bank. Available at: www.worldbank.org/safetynets

MISSING DIMENSION

Social Protection for Women Workers

With special reference to unpaid domestic workers

INDIRA HIRWAY

CONCEPT OF SOCIAL SECURITY

The concept of social security has expanded radically in terms of its content and coverage during the past few decades. The ILO Convention 102 (1952) on the Minimum Standards of Social Security for workers and elderly encompasses areas such as health care for chronic illness (HIV/AIDS, malaria and TB), sickness, old age, unemployment, employment injury, maternity benefits, family and child support, disability, and benefits for survivors and orphans (ILO 1952). However, over the years, not only the content but also the approach to social security has changed considerably.

Firstly, social security has been extended to include a variety of workers and producers, such as informal (casual and contract) workers; subsistence workers including gatherers of forest produce, water, fodder, etc; the self employed; sex workers, bonded labor, migrant workers and construction workers; and Dalits, minorities, etc.

Secondly, the concept has expanded from the idea of risk to the idea of need. This includes basic human needs, such as nutrition, shelter, health care, child care, care of the destitute, the old and disabled, etc. Social security is now seen as a tool to reduce poverty and address social exclusion, social insecurity and lack of safety. Social security is also expected to address vulnerabilities of different kinds and deprivations of different groups.

Thirdly, social security is now seen from the human rights perspective. As has been pointed out by the ILO Recommendation 202 on Social Security Floor—the Minimum Package of Social Security on Social Security Floor—the Minimum Package of Social Security (ILO 2012), social security (floor) is now a human right—all human beings, irrespective of their caste, creed, race, gender and age are entitled to the minimum floor of social protection. In addition, it is accepted that social security, along with promoting employment, is also an economic and social necessity for development and progress; that is, social security is not independent of the economic development process, but is a part of the process of development.

Finally, the delivery of social security is being viewed differently. It is now accepted that social security has to be universal, adequate, predictable and non-discriminatory. Its delivery should be transparent and accountable as well as efficient. It should also be easily accessible. The social security floor should be achieved through progressive realization with a time-bound program (ILO 2012).

In short, the paradigm of social security has changed in multiple ways. The minimum package of social security is now expected to cover inequalities, vulnerabilities, risks and uncertainties as well as promotion of capabilities and development.

Gender Dimension of Social Security

These changes are also being reflected in the gender dimension of social security. It is clear that the social security needs of men and women are different. The assumption that taking care of a household automatically includes all the members of the household is no more acceptable. There are no gender neutral policies and therefore, the social security of women is to be viewed independently and separately.

Women's human rights need to be viewed in the context of the Convention on the Elimination of all Forms of Discrimination against Women (CEDAW), an international treaty adopted in 1979 by the United Nations General Assembly; International Covenant on Economic, Social and Cultural Rights Adopted and opened for signature, ratification and accession by General Assembly resolution 2200A and UN Human Rights Declaration. Women's social security measures need to address the unequal power relations between men and women, the multiple discriminations in different fields, and gender-based vulnerabilities of women.

In spite of these radical changes in the concept and coverage of social security, it seems that the thinking as well as policies and programs related to it have not yet managed to adequately address the interests of women. For example, the Recommendation 202 on Social Protection Floors (2012) reflects almost the latest thinking on social security by the ILO. Though this recommendation has accepted a wider role of social security and sees it as an investment in people that empowers them as well as acts as a social and economic stabilizer, it does not sufficiently deal with women's vulnerabilities. It sees social security as a strategy that stimulates aggregate demand and promotes economic development, but it does not recognize women as workers if they are engaged only in unpaid domestic services. While it covers social security for pregnant women, mothers and children, it does not address the inbuilt inequalities between men and women in the labor market as well as at home. Even those with progressive views about the social sector have frequently paid inadequate attention to the needs of women in the field of social security, failing to look at issues of unequal power relations, unequal wages and vulnerabilities faced by women.

SOCIAL SECURITY NEEDS OF UNPAID DOMESTIC WORKERS

To start with, it is important to treat unpaid service work as part of economic work. The UN System of National Accounts has already accepted this as economic work (UN 2008), on the grounds that the production of unpaid services contributes to the overall well-being of people in the economy. However, these unpaid domestic services are kept outside the 'production boundary', that is, national income accounts, only for convenience and not as a concept.[1]

To put it differently, the work covered under the 'production boundary' (SNA work) and the work covered under the 'general production boundary' but outside the production boundary (non-SNA work) are interlinked in multiple ways. An activity that falls under SNA can shift to non-SNA status or vice versa, under different macro-economic conditions. For example, in a relatively prosperous economy, a considerable number of services fall under SNA (for example, cooking, cleaning, child care), while the same services would be considered non-SNA in poor countries. Also, during an economic slump several services shift to unpaid status from SNA status along with a fall in employment and incomes. The converse will be true during a boom period. This implies that macro-economic policies impact both SNA as well as non-SNA work, but differently. A clear implication of these linkages is that social security should cover the vulnerability and uncertainties of unpaid workers as well.

---

[1] The demarcation line between the SNA and non-SNA is arbitrary. In fact, the production boundary has expanded over the years to cover now all non-market production of goods. The only economic activity left under non-SNA is at present production of services for own consumption of households.

Unpaid workers, who are mainly women, suffer from a large number of vulnerabilities. These need to be addressed through a set of suitable social security measures. Time-use surveys in several countries have thrown light on these vulnerabilities.

To start with, unpaid workers engaged in domestic services usually suffer from a huge burden of overwork. Though women participate in paid work (SNA), their participation in terms of number and time is less than that of men. However, their participation in unpaid work is usually multifold as compared to men. As a result, women usually carry a much higher burden of total work than men (Hirway, 2010; Antonopoulos, 2010). Many of them, including women from non-poor households, suffer from extreme time stress and time poverty (Blackden and Wodern, 2006; Charmes, 2006; Ker and Swaminathan, 2006; Hirway, 2010).

Second, since such workers carry a disproportionately high burden of unpaid work, they have some additional disadvantages. The highly unequal distribution of unpaid work as well as the social norms attached to the distribution (first responsibility towards domestic responsibility, poor mobility, lesser access to education and health facilities, etc.) result in the overall inferior status of women in the labor market. The burden of unpaid work on women does not allow for a level-playing field in the labor market. As a result, one observes that women's work participation rates in the labor market are lower; their mobility (upward and horizontal) is much less than that of men; their human capital formation (education, skill training) is much lower and they are overcrowd in low productivity low wage sectors; women's unemployment rates are higher than that of men; and there is a gender gap in wages as well as in the other terms of employment in the labor market. Women pay a huge price for undertaking the burden of unpaid work. It is clear that unpaid workers are the lagging section of the total workforce in the economy.

In addition, unpaid workers also suffer from many disadvantages as unpaid workers. This is because the work they perform is repetitive and boring. They are usually engaged in low productivity activities and in drudgery in many cases. There is no upward mobility in this work, and there is no retirement or retirement benefits. Also, these workers, who usually remain within the four walls of their home, do not get much exposure to the outside world to widen their vision of life. Overall, unpaid workers have lower opportunities in life as workers.

In short, unpaid workers, mainly women, suffer from built-in limitations in life. This is not only unfair and unjust, but it is a clear case of violation of basic human rights.

One can state that the unequal distribution of unpaid (and paid) work between men and women is at the root of all pervasive gender inequalities and the unequal power relationship between men and women.

What kind of social protection and social security is needed to address this unjust and unequal distribution of work and power?

Pension and retirement benefits: It is frequently argued that women should be given some compensation for their work. Different proposals have been made by scholars and even policy makers in this context. One suggestion has been proposed by the Wages for Housework campaign, under which a plea has been made to give some wages to women for their work. Selma James founded International Wages for Housework Campaign in Italy in 1972. This campaign demanded 'social wages' for women for their social contribution of producing and nurturing children (to make them responsible citizens), for taking care of labor (their wear and tear), and for caring for the sick, old and other household members.

Another demand that has been made is for 'time-off for women' or a 'day-off in a week' for them, like other workers in the labor market get. Compensation to women for their 'second shift' (in addition to labor market work) or for their care work has been another demand made for unpaid workers. Pointing out 'the leisure gap' between men and women, some activists have also demanded special compensation for women. There has been a demand for 'egalitarian' families where the total work is shared by both men and women.

A problem with the above demands is that except for the last demand they all accept women's role as unpaid workers. That is, they agree with the unfair distribution of paid and unpaid work between men and women in the economy, and demand compensation for women for doing this work. In addition, there are several conceptual confusions underlying these suggestions: Is the work done for the household or for the economy? Who should pay women for their unpaid work? How much should they be paid and how does one determine the payments for women of different socio-economic groups? All these issues await resolution. Also, there is no agreement on how much to pay if the state has to pay retirement benefits to women.

Social security for unpaid workers: It has been argued by several experts now that the social security for unpaid workers should be such that it addresses the unjust division of work and moves towards gender equality and enhances women's empowerment. Rather than trying to provide monetary compensation, a better way would be to address this work and workers upfront. We make the following suggestions in this context:

Make the work visible: The first task will be to understand the dimensions and nature of this work by making it statistically visible. The only survey technique available to us for the purpose is time-use surveys. It will be necessary to mainstream time-use surveys in national statistical systems to make this work visible. This implies (1) conducting time-use surveys periodically (every five to seven years) at regular intervals; (2)

disseminate these data to all concerned government ministries/ departments (labor, women's development, planning, agriculture, industry, etc.) and to concerned outside agencies, namely academic organizations and civil society organizations; and (3) use the data in national policy making—in addressing unpaid work as well as in national/sub-national reports and policies related to poverty, employment, etc. Knowledge about the nature of unpaid services will help in designing policies to address this work.

Giving visibility to unpaid work will also imply compiling satellite accounts of this work in monetary terms so as to make visible the contribution of women's (and men's) unpaid work to GDP of the country. These figures in various countries have shown that unpaid work contributes about 30–50% of the GDP. An important implication will be that unpaid workers have a claim on the public exchequer and the government should spend these amounts for the well being of these workers.

Reduction in unpaid work: Since unpaid work is of low productivity, low income and frequent drudgery, the next strategy will be to reduce this work in the economy. This can be done mainly in two ways: (a) improving technology to reduce the drudgery element, and (b) providing infrastructure to make the work less time consuming and easy. The first way will include steps like providing fuel-efficient stoves (i.e., smokeless stoves where the requirement of fuelwood is radically reduced) or providing cooking gas or kerosene, while the second approach will include providing basic needs such as drinking water, sanitation, etc. at the doorstep.

The overall reduction in unpaid work will reduce the time stress and time poverty of women, increase their leisure time, and allow them to use their time in productive activities in the labor market.

Reducing unpaid work by transferring it to the mainstream economy: Unpaid services such as child care, care of the sick and disabled, etc. can be shifted to the mainstream economy to a considerable extent by government policy/program interventions. Governments can provide these services in the mainstream economy free or at subsidized costs. This will increase productive employment opportunities in the mainstream economy. In other words, these services can be treated as 'hidden vacancies', which can be filled by government interventions. This will not only relieve women for leisure, productive work or some other work of their choice, but it will ensure professional care for children, the old, disabled, chronically sick, etc.

Promotion of sharing of unpaid work within households: One more way of reducing the burden of unpaid work on women is to promote the sharing of unpaid work (whatever is left after the above steps) between men and women within the household. Improved sharing of work will have a significant positive impact on gender relations and women's empowerment. It will not be out of place here to observe that sharing of unpaid work by men and women will be one of the most important strategies to address the subordinate status of women at home and in the labor market.

The equal sharing of domestic services by men and women, or altering the social norms that operate behind this division of labor are difficult to achieve in the short run. However, incentives can be designed for the purpose.[2] In short, social security for unpaid workers needs to be understood from the right perspective.

---

[2] Some of these incentives could be enhancement of asset ownership by women, special programs for women's education and training and employment of women. This, however, does need major social change, such as a shift to the democratic family structure.

Integrating Unpaid Work into Macroeconomic Policies

Finally, it is important to note that social security measures cannot go all the way to address gender equality and empowerment of unpaid women workers. This task requires suitable macro-economic policies.

As seen above, it is necessary to expand the purview of macro-economics to incorporate unpaid work into it. Once this is done, macro-economic policies will take care of improving the productivity, efficiency and well-being of paid and unpaid workers.

References

Antonopoulos, Rania and Hirway, Indira (2010), 'Unpaid work and the economy: Gender, time use and poverty', in Antonopoulos, Rania and Hirway, Indira (eds), *Unpaid Work and the Economy: Gender, Time Use and Poverty in the Global South*, UK: Palgrave.

Bardasi, Elena and Wodon, Quentin (2000), 'Poverty reduction from full employment: A time-use approach', USA: World Bank

Bardasi, Elena and Woden, Quentin (2006), 'Measuring time poverty and analyzing its determinants: Concepts and application to Guinea', USA: World Bank

Blackden, Mark and Wodon, Quentin (2006), 'Gender, time-use, and poverty in sub-Saharan Africa', USA: World Bank

Charmes, J. (2006), 'Gender and time poverty in sub-Saharan Africa: A review of empirical evidence', in Blackden, M. and Wodon, Q. (eds), *Gender, Time Use and Poverty in Sub-Saharan Africa*, World Bank Working Paper.

Hirway, Indira (2010), 'Understanding poverty: Insights emerging from the time use of the poor', in Rania, Antonopoulos and Hirway, Indira (eds), *Unpaid Work and the Economy: Gender, Time Use and Poverty in the Global South*, UK: Palgrave.

International Labour Organization (ILO) (1952), Convention 102 on Social Security (the Minimum Standards), ILO, Geneva.

International Labour Organization (ILO) (2012), Recommendation 202 on Social Security (the Minimum Standards), ILO, Geneva.

Women's Invisibility as Workers

Aasha Kapur Mehta

INTRODUCTION AND CONTEXT*

For several reasons, there are serious inaccuracies in the recording of work contributed by women in India. This is not a new issue and has been highlighted by several researchers and activists since at least the 1970s. However, the problem has still not been adequately addressed. Since data is the foundation on which policy is built, any flaws in the data will lead to flaws in policy based on it. Hence, the importance of the accurate counting of women workers.

This chapter aims to highlight three issues in the context of the invisibility of work contributed by women:

i. Under-reporting or non-reporting of women's work, thereby rendering it invisible.
ii. Deviations between NSS estimates presented in the Reports on Key Indicators of Employment and Unemployment

---

* This essay builds on a background paper on Women and the Economy in India for *The South Asian Human Development Report, 2000* and on Aasha Kapur Mehta "The Invisible Workers: Women's Unrecognised Contribution to the Economy", *Manushi*, November-December, 2000.

in India and other documents based on these surveys and the NSS Report No. 550 on Participation of Women in Specified Activities along with Domestic Duties, 2009–10.

iii. Unpaid care work that is neither recognized nor included in estimates of GDP.

These issues have been discussed using Maithreyi Krishnaraj's (1990) categorization of women's work in rural and urban areas:

i. Wage and salaried employment
ii. Self-employment outside the household for profit
iii. Self-employment in cultivation and household industry for profit
iv. Self-employment in cultivation for own consumption
v. Other subsistence activities in allied sectors like dairying, rearing of livestock such as poultry, goats, pigs, etc., and fishing, hunting and cultivation of fruit and vegetable gardens
vi. Activities related to domestic work, such as fetching fuel, fodder, water, forest produce, repair of dwellings, making cow dung-cakes, food preservation, etc.
vii. Domestic work such as cooking, cleaning, taking care of children, the aged and the sick

The work contributed by women and women workers in categories (i) and (ii) is included in estimates of women workers as well as in estimates of National Income or NNP at factor cost or GDP at market prices. However, what is invisible, and therefore goes unrecognized, is the fact that women workers make a vast contribution to the output produced by family farms, through animal husbandry, collection of forest produce, etc. While the output may be included in estimates of the National Income calculated on the basis of the output method, the women themselves are not counted as workers. Several micro-studies conducted since the 1970s provide detailed estimates of measurement failure and the invisibilization of women's contributions to items (iii), (iv) and (v). Item (vi) is concerned with activities relating to agricultural production, like maintenance of kitchen gardens, work in household poultry, dairy, processing of primary goods produced by households for their own consumption, etc. These issues are discussed in Section III. Item (vii), care work, is not included in estimates of GDP as it is outside the purview of the System of National Accounts. This is briefly discussed in Section IV. Section V concludes the chapter.

Under-reporting or Non-reporting of Women's Work: Evidence from Literature

Numerous micro-studies have recorded estimates of measurement failure. Despite clear evidence from such studies and considerable efforts by scholars and activists to raise these issues as well as sensitize data producers, women's work is not accurately captured. Several attempts have been made to identify errors in the measuring of the number of women workers. Important findings from a few of these are outlined below.

One such survey was conducted by Devaki Jain and Malini Chand (Jain and Chand, 1982) covering households in six villages—three in Bharatpur district of Rajasthan and three in Birbhum district of West Bengal, between September 1976 and December 1977. The total sample size was 127 households, of which 52 were in Rajasthan and 75 in West Bengal. The critical point to be noted is that the mode of investigation was observation and not recall. Each selected household was observed over two consecutive days, when the activities of every member of age five and above were recorded for a period of 15 hours, between 6.00 a.m. and 9.00 p.m. The frequency of observation of each small household was once in two months, i.e., six times during the 52-week cycle. Comparing the data obtained from the census of households and the time allocation data for the same household, Jain and Chand's findings were as follows:

i. In Rajasthan, four out of the 37 women reported as non-workers in the schedule were, in fact, spending up to four hours a day in activities such as groundnut-picking and sowing the field. Nine others who were reported as non-workers were grazing cattle and cutting grass for more than one hour per day. Thus, 13 out of 37, i.e., at least 30%, were outside the questionnaire net. Two of the 36 male children and two of the 34 female children who were reported as non-workers were observed to be hoeing the fields; 18 other female children were grazing cattle and cutting grass.
ii. In West Bengal, 20 out of 104 females who reported themselves as non-workers were observed to be engaged in activities such as winnowing, threshing and parboiling, working as domestic servants in the homes of others for as many as 8–10 hours per day. This indicates the seriousness of measurement failure.
iii. The gainful activity of females and children—the tasks they engage in, their location—is not recognized under the existing investigation methodology with the same precision as their male counterparts.
iv. During harvest or any other peak farm income activity in rural households, there is the additional work of feeding farm hands (own and hired). The processing of grain, cooking, and serving/washing involved in feeding them is usually done by women. This is not counted as work.

Concerned about the 'countless generalizations' about women's work participation based on official census statistics and the deviations of this data from her own observations as well as those of others, Gail Omvedt (1992) showed that there were a total of 239 women workers in one village where the

1971 Census had counted only 39, and 444 workers in a second village where only nine appeared in the census.

> It is not that this work was 'invisible' in any literal sense, or that it was work done in the house out of sight of census takers. In fact, going to these villages after 10:30–11:00 a.m. for survey work was impossible because the vast majority of the women were in the fields and not in their houses. Yet their work was socially invisible; the census simply did not count these women as 'workers'. Perhaps the greatest injustice is done to peasant women. Their 'work participation' is said to be small and to be declining. Yet from the Jawari areas of Maharashtra to the rice regions of South and East India, the hill economy of the north west and the Adivasi areas of South Bihar, there is evidence that women work as hard or harder than men in agriculture. Perhaps it is time we simply threw away the census data and recognized that a substantial portion of the field work and almost all supplementary work (care of dairy animals, grain processing, etc.) is done by women of peasant families in addition to child-care and cooking chores.

She draws the conclusion that:

> [I]n agriculture and in almost all of the unorganized sectors (organized sector work data, for obvious reasons, are relatively more accurate) women work harder than men—particularly when all forms of 'subsistence production' are included—whether or not this is reflected in the census data. Above all, we cannot, at this point, accept any generalizations regarding women's 'declining work participation' as a result of overall economic trends.

In an attempt to compensate for the socially generated 'invisibility' of women's work, Omvedt (1992) estimated a total of 80–100 million uncounted women workers in 1981.

Attributing the continued invisibility of women's work to 'deeply entrenched social customs, taboos and prejudices', the Report of the National Commission on self employed women and women in the Informal Sector or the Shramshakti (1998) report observes that the average hours of unpaid work by married women outside the home vary from 6.13 to 7.53 hours per day, some of them working more than 10 hours each day. Apart from domestic duties, women who are engaged in agricultural operations spend an average of about 12 hours on the farm and in taking care of cattle at home.

In the context of work participation rates in Punjab, Ratna Sudarshan (1998) found that while the 1991 Census reported the female work force participation rate (FWPR) at 4.4%, the National Council of Applied Economic Research (NCAER) survey, which included follow up probing questions, reported an estimate of 28.8%. Similar observations have been made in other micro-studies. Prem Chowdhary (1994) explains that animal-related tasks include bringing fodder from the fields, chaff-cutting, preparing feed mix for the cattle, giving water and feeding, bathing and cleaning the cattle, cleaning the cattle shed, treating sick cattle, making dung cakes, preparing structures for storing dry dung cakes and compost making. 'Despite all this work, so far as the recognition of their contribution to dairy farming is concerned, women again remain invisible. A 1973 inquiry into the dairy development program in Ambala district reported that no female was declared to be a worker in the animal husbandry work.'

According to Sardamoni (1987),

> ...where men and women work jointly, it was found that women got up early in the morning, cut the ripened crop and made the bundles. The men got up later and carried the bundles to the threshing yard. The women then helped in the threshing and winnowing but did not wait for the grain

to be measured and payment [to be] received as they had to rush to make small purchases and cook for the night.

Therefore, in cases where men and women work together, the work contributed by women gets subsumed under household activity and their contribution as workers is invisibilized.

In several states in India, tribals collect valuable non-timber forest produce (NTFP) or minor forest produce, for which they receive exploitatively low returns. As can be seen from the activity profile and gender-wise distribution of tasks listed in Table 1 below, women's contribution to the collection of NTFP such as gum is significant in a large number of tasks. Yet their role remains invisible. For instance, in order to collect gum karaya, tribal men and women walk for about 6–10 km to reach the forest, where each family has clearly earmarked trees. Blazing or injuring the tree in order to produce gum is generally done by the men. During a field visit to Rajavomangi and discussions with 14 women gum pickers in one village, it was learnt that one of the women (not present at the meeting), who was a widow, blazed trees on her own.

Table 1: Activity profile and gender-wise distribution of tasks

Activity	Female	Male
Planting trees and forest protection	X	X
Walk to tree	X	X
First blaze		Xxxx
Second or third blaze	X	Xxxx
Collecting gum	X	X
Carrying baskets	X	X
Cleaning with forceps	Xxxx	
Drying	Xxxx	
Grading and sorting for storage	Xxxx	
Making bamboo platforms		X

Activity	Female	Male
Travelling to the shandy	x	X
Checking weight and grade	x	Xxxx
Selling or receiving payment at shandy	x	X

Source: Aasha Kapur Mehta, Women's Economic Empowerment in The Asia Pacific Region: Report on Gum Karaya, India, UNIFEM SARO based on discussions with Shri Vijay Kumar, Dr. M.V. Rao, Kovel and 14 women gum pickers in Kovelpuram village.

Most women accompany their husbands to the forest and carry baskets and clear the path. While the male member of the family blazes the trees, the women collect leafy vegetables, twigs, tubers, shoots, etc. On each visit to the forest, they collect gum and also make fresh blazes where needed. Trips for gum collection are made thrice every week. On returning to the village, the women place the gum on an elevated platform for drying, ensure that the different sides of gum dry uniformly, remove the bark, wood and other foreign matter, and then grade and sort the gum before storing it. The process of cleaning, sorting, grading, and drying the gum takes about four to five days. It is then taken to the collection point at the shandy, where an inspector weighs it and pays for it. Women contribute to almost all the tasks prior to the actual weighing and payment. Yet their contribution to the collection and processing of gum karaya remains unrecognized.

Mencher and Sardamoni (1982) refer to the Second Agricultural Labour Enquiry Report, which notes that the agricultural operations that women were mostly employed in include weeding, transplanting and harvesting and that 'they were seldom employed in strenuous operations like ploughing'. Questioning the assumption that all female jobs need less strength, Mencher and Sardamoni quote a male anthropologist who reported that when he asked a man why males did not do transplanting and weeding work, he was told, 'No man can keep standing bent over all day long in the mud and rain. It is much too difficult, and our backs would hurt too much.' It is well known that women transplant and weed and perform a large number of tasks that constitute 'productive' economic activity.

In 1998–99, a Pilot Time Use Survey was conducted by the Ministry of Statistics and Programme Implementation, covering 18,591 households spread over six selected states. The survey showed that if we take System of National Accounts (SNA) and extended SNA activities together, the average time spent by rural males is only 46.05 hours, as compared to 56.48 hours by rural females. For urban males, this figure comes to 44.50 hours, as compared to 45.60 hours by urban females.

Reasons for the Statistical Invisibility of Women in the National Accounts

Why is the contribution of women to the economy unrecorded, unrecognized or statistically invisible within the framework of the national accounting system? The Shramshakti report points out that although women play the dual role of reproduction and production, their contribution is considered 'secondary', 'marginal' and 'supplementary'. Even when they do vital preparatory work as in weaving, agriculture and pottery, they are at best acknowledged as 'helpers'. This under-valuation is all-pervasive.

Numerous reasons have been cited so far for the under-reporting of women's work. These include methodological problems pertaining to investigation, biases stemming from definitions used, measurement failure, the nature and style of women's work, the difficulty of classifying the activities women engage in because of their sheer range, the dominance of domestic work leading to under-reporting of other work, convention, the unpaid nature of their work, the misperception of female economic roles by respondents, biases of interviewers/

enumerators, intermingling of production for self-consumption with production for sale, cultural/ideological systems, lack of recognition of the multidimensional functions of women, the fact that they contribute to family economic activities resulting in their personal contributions being merged with those of the family, whereby their work is rendered invisible. Some of these reasons are documented below in more detail.

- The failure of the existing investigation methodology to capture the gainful activity and tasks that females and children engage in with the same precision as is done in the case of males (Jain and Chand, 1982).
- Factors such as (i) quality and/or biases of interviewers; (ii) biases of male respondents and/or lack of knowledge on the part of proxy-respondents; (iii) poorly constructed questionnaires; (iv) ambiguous and ill-understood definitions of labor force participation (Anker, Khan and Gupta, 1998).
- Information is usually obtained from the male head of household. In a cultural setting where women's involvement in anything other than domestic work is considered disreputable, this leads to the underestimation of women's participation in non-domestic work, especially outside the home (Agarwal).
- Since rural Indian women typically engage in a variety of labor force activities, each for a relatively small amount of time, classifications based on one main activity alone—as is usually the case at present—are inappropriate (Anker, Khan and Gupta, 1998).
- The tendency of women to identify themselves as 'only housewives' even when they are economically active, reflects a common cultural pattern in many developing nations. Unless questions are formulated with sufficient care, there is a strong likelihood of a woman underestimating the economically productive content of her work, insofar as she herself

considers it a part of 'domestic duties' and reports it as such (Agarwal).
- The dominance of domestic work does lead to the under-reporting of other work (Jain and Chand, 1982).
- Women spend several hours each day working and/or supervising work within the household. The National Income Accounts do not reflect work done within the household 'due to convention and problems of measurement. Since much of the work within the household is done by women, their contribution to the economy is rendered invisible' (Kulshreshtha and Singh).
- Work styles of women are determined by history, biology, attitudes—a whole package. These work styles are characterized by intermittent participation over the life cycle of women as well as during each day, contributing to a productive activity but at the processing/pre-marketing and less visible monetized stage. The intermingling of production for self-consumption with production for sale is not an easy problem to solve, and existing designs do not address this challenge (Jain and Chand, 1982).
- Women of poor rural households are routinely involved in manual work related to cultivation and processing, in addition to their work in the fields. Most peasant women engage in a significant proportion of the work involved in pre- and post-harvest operations that are carried out in the home compound. The working day of a poor woman in India may last between 12 and 16 hours. The invisibility of women's work, domestic chores and other tasks is part of a cultural/ideological system that views man as the primary bread-winner (Duvvury, 1989).
- Women report themselves as non-workers because they tend to regard their activities as 'domestic responsibilities' and therefore outside market related or remunerated work (Krishnaraj, 1990).

- Indian women are engaged in two kinds of work: one that produces an income and the other that does not. The former in turn has home-based work and work outside the home. Even within the latter, there are many components that are not 'pure' domestic work like cooking, cleaning, child care, but include post-harvest processing, livestock maintenance, gathering of fuel, fodder, water and forest produce, unpaid family labor in the family farm or family enterprise, and so on (Krishnaraj, 1990).
- In the non-market sector, where most women work, the distinction between economic and non-economic activities is seldom clear and most arbitrarily applied. Among the poor in developing nations, virtually all adults and sizeable numbers of children engage in 'economic activities' in order to help the family meet its basic needs. Much of this work occurs outside the marketplace (Krishnaraj 1990).
- A striking example of the significant influence of perception on measurement is indicated by a small survey commissioned by UNIFEM, India, which found that 98 out of 100 enumerators did not even put the question regarding work to women; it was simply assumed by them that they did not work. In other words, out of 2002 women in the 1000 households covered, only four women were actually asked any question about the work they had done in the past year (SARH and SCOPE, 1996).
- Poor women are invariably involved in economic activities, but when these are related to family occupations like agriculture, animal husbandry, forestry, weaving, construction labor and cottage industries, their personal contributions gets merged with that of the family and becomes invisible (Shramshakti, 1998).
- Given the prevailing cultural norms whereby a woman doing manual work outside the house is associated with low social

status, the male head of the household usually identifies the woman as a housewife and non-worker (Visaria, 1999).

Deviations between NSS estimates

Deviations between NSS estimates presented in the Reports on Key Indicators of Employment and Unemployment in India, and other documents based on these surveys in the Employment and Unemployment Report, and the NSS Reports on Participation of Women in Specified Activities along with Domestic Duties

The National Sample Survey and Workforce Participation Rate

Despite improvements, the female-worker-population ratio or work force participation rates of women are hindered by the under-reporting of women's work. Over all the NSS large sample rounds between 1973–74 and 2009–10, while the worker population ratio for males has uniformly been more than 50% in both rural and urban areas, the corresponding estimate for females has varied between 26% and 34% for rural areas and 13.4% and 16.6% for urban areas. In the fifth quinquennial survey on employment and unemployment in its 50th round (1993–94), the NSS reported information regarding the participation of women in household work and other specified household activities, which resulted in economic benefits to their households (Sarvekshana, 1997). Each person categorized as usually engaged in household duties in the principal status was asked whether he/she pursued certain specified activities more or less regularly for household consumption along with his/her normal household chores. These activities were grouped into three broad categories:

i. Activities relating to agricultural production like maintenance of kitchen garden, work in household poultry, dairy, etc., including free collection of agricultural products for household consumption.
ii. Processing of primary products produced by the household for household consumption.
iii. Other activities for own consumption, but which result in economic benefits to the household.

During 1993–94, about 29% of rural women and 42% of urban women in India were found to be usually (principal and subsidiary) engaged only in household duties. Each person categorized as usually engaged in household duties in terms of principal status was asked whether they pursued certain specific activities, listed under categories (i) to (iii) above, more or less regularly for household consumption, along with normal household chores.

In this context, the NSS 1993–94 household survey reported that 29% of rural women and 42% of urban women were engaged only in household work and were without work even in the subsidiary status. Subsequently, it was noted that 58% of women characterized in this way in rural areas and 14% in urban areas were actually involved in maintaining kitchen gardens, household poultry, collecting fish, collecting firewood, husking paddy, grinding food-grains, preserving meat, preparing gur, making baskets, etc.. In other words they were engaged in economic activities. NSS calculates the percentage of such women, incorrectly categorized as 'not working', as 17% in rural areas and 5.8% in urban areas. Hence, the Worker Population Ratio (WPR) for women should be raised by adding 17% and 5.8% respectively to the WPR for women of 32.8% in rural and 15.5% in urban areas for 1993–94.

Table 2: Workforce participation rate

Year	Rural		Urban	
	Female	Male	Female	Male
1972–73	31.8	54.5	13.4	50.1
1977–78	33.1	55.2	15.6	50.8
1983	34.0	54.7	15.1	51.2
1987–88	32.3	53.9	15.2	50.6
1993–94	32.8	55.3	15.5	52.1
1993–94 revised to include NSS estimates of women incorrectly categorised as not working	49.8		21.3	
1999–2000	29.9	53.1	13.9	51.8
2004–5	32.7	54.6	16.6	54.9
2009–10	26.1	54.7	13.8	54.3
2009–10 revised include NSS estimates of women incorrectly categorized as not working (based on Report 550)	45.3		22.6	

Source: National Sample Survey Office
Note: Figures for all the years are based on usual status approach and include principal status and subsidiary status workers of all ages.

Further, in 2009–10, the Worker Population Ratio (WPR) for women, based on the usual status approach (considering both principal activity and subsidiary activity), in rural and urban areas was 26.1% and 13.8%, respectively (see Table 2, second last row). The NSS Report No. 550 on Participation of Women in Specified Activities along with Domestic Duties, 2009–10 found that about 56% of the women in rural areas and 19% in urban areas pursue one or more of the activities under categories (i) and (ii), along with their domestic chores, for household consumption.

> If all women usually engaged in economic activities, irrespective of their intensity of participation and even considering those included within the extended production boundary according to SNA-2008, are to be considered to be 'workers' to arrive at an approximate upper bound to the usual status women 'workers', then 19.2% in rural areas and 8.8% in urban areas could be added to the usual status worker population ratio for women.

In other words, 'the upper bound of the WPR of women is 45.3% in rural areas and 22.6% in urban areas'. However, NSS does not take the logical next step and make the correction.

Care Work

Care work at home is not considered to be work. According to the NSS Report No. 550 on Participation of Women in Specified Activities along with Domestic Duties, 2009–10, at the all-India level, 'the proportion of persons engaged *in domestic duties* in the usual principal status, was 42.2% among females but only 0.5% among males.' The Pilot Time Use Survey mentioned above showed that females spent about double the time as compared to males in activities relating to taking care of children, sick and elderly people. The lack of leisure time in women's lives because of their responsibilities such as cooking, cleaning, child care and caring for the aged, in addition to all the other tasks that they perform, has an impact on women's health. There is immense emotional trauma and drudgery associated with caring for the sick, aged and disabled. While most women perform these tasks, care work requires recognition and support from the state, at the very least in the form of support and skills for home-based care.

Conclusions

There are serious inaccuracies and measurement failure in the recording of the contributions women make through the work that they do. Several reasons for this have been outlined in Section II. Women are known to work longer hours than men and the fact is that women participate in the work force to a far greater extent than is currently being recorded.

The efforts of researchers and activists since the 1970s met with partial success with the NSSO following up with probing questions on those who were reportedly engaged in domestic duties in 1993–94; it was then noted that such women—incorrectly categorized as 'not working'—constituted 17% of women in rural areas and 5.8% in urban areas.

The NSS uses activity codes for determining which activities are counted as work and which are not. A person who attended to domestic duties only is assigned activity code 92 and a person who mainly attended domestic duties and was also simultaneously engaged in free collection of primary goods (vegetables, roots, firewood, cattle-feed, etc.), sewing, tailoring, weaving, making baskets and mats, etc., for household use, in his/her usual principal status, is assigned activity code 93. As a result of their probing questions, NSS has estimated that '19.2% in rural areas and 8.8% in urban areas, could be added to the usual status worker population ratio for women'. In other words, WPR for women in 2009–10 would be 45.3% (and not 26.1%) in rural areas, and 22.6% (as opposed to 13.8%) in urban areas.

While this is a huge step forward, for the contribution of women as workers to become truly visible, it is important that NSS takes the logical next step and adds the results of the probing questions based on responses to activity codes 92 and 93 to the estimates of WPR for women presented in all the reports on Key Indicators of Employment and Unemployment in India and other documents based on these surveys, instead of only publishing them in a separate report regarding the participation of women in specified activities along with domestic duties.

References

Agarwal, Bina (1985), 'Work participation of rural women in third world: Some data and conceptual biases', *Economic and Political Weekly*, p. A-156.

Anker, Richard, Khan, M. E. and Gupta, R. B. (1998), 'Women's participation in the labour force: A methods test in India for improving its measurement', *Women, Work, and Development* 16, Geneva: International Labour Organization.

Chowdhry, Prem (1994), 'High participation, low evaluation: Women and work in rural Haryana', *Economic and Political Weekly*, pp. A-140–141.

Duvvury, Nata (1989), 'Women in agriculture: A review of Indian literature', *Economic and Political Weekly*, 28 October 1989, p. WS-97.

Jain, Devaki and Chand, Malini (1982), 'Report on a time allocation study: Its methodological implications', Technical Seminar on Women's Work and Employment 9–11 April 1982, Institute of Social Studies Trust.

Krishnaraj, Maithreyi (1990), 'Women's work in Indian census: Beginnings of change', *Economic and Political Weekly*, 1–8 December.

Mencher, J.P. and Sardamoni, K. (1982), 'Muddy feet, dirty hands', *Economic and Political Weekly*, December 1982, pp. A-151–152.

Omvedt, Gail (1992), 'The "unorganised sector" and women workers', *Guru Nanak Journal of Sociology*, Vol. 13(I), April 1992, pp. 19–61.

Sardamoni, K. (1987), 'Labour, land and rice production', *Economic and Political Weekly*, April 1987, p. WS 3.

Sudarshan, Ratna M. (1998), 'Employment of women, trends and characteristics', National Seminar on in Search of New Vistas, Women's Vocational Training Programme, Directorate General of Employment and Training, 30–31 July 1998, New Delhi.

Visaria, Pravin (1999), 'Level and pattern of female employment, 1911–1994', in Papola, T.S. and Sharma, Alakh, N., eds, *Gender and Employment in India*, New Delhi: Vikas Publishing House, p. 23.

——— (1997), 'A note on participation of Indian women in household work and other specified activities, 1993–94', *Sarvekshana*, October–December 1997.

——— (1998), 'Shramshakti: Report of the National Commission on self employed women and women in the Informal Sector', National Commission on Self Employed Women and Women in the Informal Sector, June 1998, New Delhi, p. 28.

Livelihood Security Critical for Women's Social Security

Nalini Nayak

The term 'social security' means different things to different people depending on where we are located in the economic ladder in society. But according to Article 22 of the Universal Declaration of Human Rights,

> Everyone, as a member of society, has the right to social security and is entitled to realization, through national effort and international co-operation and in accordance with the organization and resources of each state, of the economic, social and cultural rights indispensable for his dignity and the free development of his personality. In simple terms, the signatories agree that society in which a person lives should help them to develop and to make the most of all the advantages (culture, work, social welfare) which are offered to them in the country.

The first part of the above extract implies that a society in which a person lives should help her/him to develop and to make the most of all the advantages, while the second part states that social security may also refer to the action programs of the government that are intended to promote the welfare of the population through assistance measures, guaranteeing access to sufficient resources for food and shelter, and promoting the health and well-being of the population at large and potentially vulnerable segments such as children, the elderly, the sick and the unemployed, in particular. Services providing social security are often called social services.

Unfortunately for us in India, we tend to focus only on the latter aspect, forgetting that it is the first part that is more important.

This essay hopes to focus on what social security means for poor women workers, small women producers who live on the margins but who are crucial in providing not only the subsistence base to over 50% of our population, but of creating a social matrix of harmony. While this may sound like one is romanticizing and idealizing the rural countryside which also poses its own share of challenges for women, it is undeniable that modern development has not rid society of its patriarchal manifestations which have only commodified all inter-personal relationships and women's bodies (not to mention the ill effects of global warming and depletion of natural resources). In utter contrast, large areas of our country, even entire states like in north-east India for example, actually depend on subsistence production in which women are the main producers of local food and other products like clothing.

As stated earlier, social security is most often equated with welfare measures and schemes to alleviate poverty. Every successive government has sought to either remodel or increase the number of welfare schemes under a variety of names. Each of these decisions is preceded by massive discussions in the parliament regarding whether the state treasuries can afford such a welfare measure or not. In other words, provisions are linked to the 'growth' figures of the economy and taxation systems. It is high time that the fallacy of such growth is confronted. In the last three to four decades, but more so in the latter two decades, the number of 'development refugees' has been on the rise. What does this mean? Various development projects promoted as so-called engines of growth have displaced people from their land either by large-scale evictions for mining or for huge infrastructure development like roads, canals and dams, or by compelling them to leave their homes in search of work by polluting land and water sources that people traditionally used for livelihood. In our great urge to forge ahead and prove to the world that India is a 'world class' nation, we have focussed on growth figures in the belief that they give the world an indication of the well-being of the nation. At the same time, we emphatically affirm that only growth can help the poor, which again is not entirely true. The growth we have seen in these last decades has mostly been about investments that leave a large section of the population marginalized and destitute. The logic behind providing welfare measures and social security schemes then seems to be to first rob people of their right to live with dignity and then pretend to offer them measly compensation without dignity.

This view runs the risk of being criticized for being 'anti-development'. Nevertheless, the economic logic which focusses only on the production of the formal sector and the market is rarely questioned. Blindly believing in the logic of the market, which time and again has taught us rude lessons, and our preoccupation with issues of the organized industry leaves us oblivious to the larger economy, which is informal for the most part. As a result there is very little data or even information in government circles regarding the production of the informal sector and the manner in which people in the informal sector survive. Even labor officers seem to know very little about the informal producers except in sectors where these workers have succeeded to organize and raise their voice. It is these millions of small producers and even subsistence producers who form an important spoke in the economic wheel, and who are mostly women, whose livelihood security is our focus in this essay.

At the outset, there are three key questions that need to be answered: what does subsistence mean; why is it important to safeguard subsistence; and what does social security for subsistence producers imply. Popular subsistence theories generally refer to subsistence wages. This is not our concern here since at present we are discussing subsistence production, i.e., communities that provide for themselves via access to the natural resource base, be it land, water or forests. These communities are often also drawn into the market for other commodities that they do not self-produce, but in this way they not only sustain large populations but also help sustain the traditional skills and culture that form the cultural matrix of our diverse country. Such communities generally have multiple skills—for instance, they may fish or grow food or collect forest produce while also engaging in other productive work like weaving, embroidery, carpentry, music, etc., and may further be available on a seasonal basis as labor. Such seasonal migrations in several sectors and in several parts of the country keep the larger production systems functional. The fishing communities in Bengal who migrate further down the river for the winter fisheries producing tonnes of dry fish for food, the agricultural workers of Madhya Pradesh who help cut sugarcane in Maharashtra or harvest crops in Punjab, the Odia workers who move to Bihar and neighboring states during the brick-making season are all examples of such seasonal migrations. This seasonal work helps communities get the added cash they require to keep their lives and livelihoods going, while staying attached to their small landholdings, sacred groves, and pristine eco-niches that add color, sound, song and dance to the varied cultural expressions in this country. What does social security mean for these millions?

One facet of social security for women in these communities has to do with securing their right of access to the natural resources that they have so long depended on. While today several modern scientists have documented customary practices and traditional knowledge, the important task that remains is to understand and document customary law. Many of these communities have always held the rights to use the natural resources, a fact recognized even by the modern state. In the case of the fisher folk of Mumbai for instance, their right to access their habitation and fishing grounds was conserved by the British law and hence, we still find the Koli villages existing alongside the modern sprawl of Mumbai. The Koli habitation was also upgraded over the years so the younger generations in the community were able to benefit from education and even make professional shifts. But a Koliwada is still a Koliwada, and the Mumbai fish market is still served by the women of the Koliwadas from far and near. As fish workers organized during the 1980s, several state governments heeded their demands and provided support systems to sustain their livelihoods—transport to go to the market, reserved wagons on the suburban trains, storage facilities, loans, etc. While much more can be done, there are now at least institutional mechanisms put in place that can respond to people's demands when called for in the fisheries sector. The Koli community is proud of their work and live with dignity. If such institutional mechanisms are well-manned and effective, livelihood support for such communities would be the best social security offered.

The umbrella legislation for the informal sector that was included in the Second Labor Commission Report provides the respect and right to natural resources established by customary law. Hence, social protection or security is a right of communities and should figure high on any democratic agenda.

In earlier decades, the government of India had created cooperatives and then various development corporations in various sectors, like the Handicrafts Development Corporation and so on, which assisted local artisans to sustain their skills and livelihoods. Some of these went on to assist in marketing and product design. These were extremely beneficial efforts and proved important in providing livelihood security to many traditional communities. Nevertheless, in several states these corporations have either become heavily bureaucratic or lifeless institutions, or have not kept abreast of the changing times, thus leaving local artisans to fend for themselves or just die natural deaths.

The other facet related to livelihood security has to do with making migration safe and decent. The right of mobility in this country is guaranteed by the constitution as we are Indian citizens. Seasonal migration for work, however, is not safeguarded, however—the channels of exploitation leading to bondage and exploitation abound. While there is an old Interstate Migrant Workers Act that was amended in 2012, the act is still wanting as it has not adapted to the changing times, and there are certainly no institutional mechanisms in place to guarantee safe and decent migration. That women who migrate with their families are also provided health and child care facilities, potable water and sanitation, and that they are not exposed to abuse is the very basis of social security. Such protective measures exist nowhere. Although India now seems to be aggressively confronting child and bonded labor, it has not had much success in this regard. MOUs between labor-sending and -receiving states are in process albeit in preliminary stages; it is imperative that these efforts receive persistent and committed government attention if the desired results are to be achieved.

The NREGA was also seen as a social security measure providing 100 days of work to a family at a fair wage. In several parts of the country it is the women in the family who apply for such work as the men generally earn a higher wage or migrate elsewhere for work. While this is certainly a boon for rural populations wherever it is implemented well, its effectiveness in creating public assets needs to be more closely examined. After the initial years, it seems that the local governments run out of ideas for engaging workers through NREGS and asset creation spills over into the private domain as well. In a country where people have a variety of traditional skills and produce local goods for use like rope, fabric, tools, woven mats, baskets and forest produce, or even terrace the lands to grow food crops, etc., giving them the NREGS wage to sustain the skill and also the product would also be a way to ensure that their livelihood is sustained. None of these traditional occupations today earn the NREGS per-day wage. 100 days of such wage work would work like a subsidy for the product that could also be bought affordably by the local consumers while the producer would be able to sustain the craft and skill. Efforts could also be made to improve productivity so that the worker may earn more money even on the non-NREGS days.

Including locally produced grain in the public distribution system (PDS) is another way to sustain local producers. It would also facilitate the consumption of food that a local population is accustomed to eating rather than turning the population of the entire country into a wheat-eating one simply because that is what agri-business suggests. If people in Karnataka prefer to eat ragi and people in Andhra eat millets, while people in Gujarat and Maharashtra eat bajra, and people in the north-east eat sticky rice and naga dhal, why should the PDS not encourage the procurement and distribution of such grains? Procurement at a smaller scale is considered to be a hazard but considering the wastage and pilferage of grain in the storehouses at present and the costs of transporting it, it may be more logical to decentralize the system in a rational manner. In fact, it is high time we paid more attention to the rationalization of the PDS rather than confining the options to mere cash transfers, which seem to be an easy and corruption-free fix. Is not food sovereignty and thereby food security the most important aspect of social security? There may be far cheaper methods to develop such systems which are diverse but inclusive. As a matter of fact, there is a great need to apply the skills of the IT age to monitor national systems while the actual nitty-gritty of procurement, storage and distribution is effectively decentralized. If the Indian Election Commission has so effectively managed to see to it that even the most isolated individual in the most secluded mountain have access to a polling booth, surely it is not impossible to make the PDS a truly life and livelihood supporting measure.

Intrinsic to the sustenance of the local production systems is the need to conserve the environment. The environment provides us with several intangible services, and therefore, the conservation of the environment is also key to sustainability. Rewarding communities for conserving ecosystem services is therefore also a social security measure. For instance, if people who live on the fringes of forests cannot grow food crops because forest animals eat them up, then they should be compensated for their food and not compelled to clear the forests. By conserving the forests they would be ensuring water retention from the rains and hence, water for consumption or cultivation downstream. These are important services that need to be conserved and therefore, rewarded. Similarly, people who live near marshlands or own marshlands should not be encouraged to fill them and then sell them as prices of land go up. Marshlands provide important eco services and should be conserved. Hence, such land owners or communities also need compensation so that they are not disadvantaged in the market economy.

Participation of women in decision-making at the level of local governance has improved, but true participation in managing their local production in ways that lighten their physical labor and reward them for their work with promises of care in old age is the real social security that the mass of women workers desire. Hence, we should be thinking of a broad framework in which social security is developed. Its focus should be on sustaining life and livelihood. It is not sufficient for the government to speak of inclusive growth. It should make a commitment to securing ongoing livelihoods and providing the wherewithal for developing them in terms of adding value and making them sustainable. The concept of growth and development itself should be rearticulated to include social security.

UNPACKING SOCIAL SECURITY

Social Pensions
The Real Aadhaar for the Niradhar
A detailed evaluation of the successes and challenges before the system of social pensions in Maharashtra

Anjor Bhaskar[*]

Context

The National Social Assistance Programme caters to the needs of some of the most vulnerable sections of our society, those who are desperately in need of support: widows, the elderly and disabled, and those who have lost the earning members of their family.

[*] This study derives its information from two sources. The first is through the direct involvement of the author with Kagad Kach Patra Kashtakari Panchayat (KKPKP) through 2011–2013. KKPKP is a union of waste pickers which has been involved in helping obtain social pensions for old and destitute waste pickers in Pune. The second is the author's involvement in the PEEP survey, which was conducted to assess the state of entitlement programs (including social pensions) in the districts of Nandurbar and Osmanabad in June 2013. The author would like to thank all the field workers, the waste pickers, the rural elderly and the destitutes who gave time and instilled their faith in me. I would also like to thank Prof. Jean Dreze and Dr. Reetika Khera for allowing me to participate in the PEEP survey, and Poornima Chikarmane who drew me into the struggle for social pensions. I hope this study is able to contribute towards better implementation of pension schemes in India.

Widows are in a particularly miserable state in India, as they not only have to deal with the loss of their husbands (who, in most cases, are the only earning members of the household) but also deal with social and cultural practices that are largely targeted against widows and impose several restrictions on their mobility and occupational choices. Through a household survey in rural areas of three states, Dreze and Srinivasan (1997) verify their hypothesis that 'even relatively small economies of scale imply that the incidence of poverty among single widows, widows living with unmarried children, and female household heads (all of whom tend to live in relatively small households) is higher than in the population as a whole' (Dreze and Srinivasan, 1997) based on National Sample Survey data on consumer expenditure. In terms of standard poverty indices based on household per-capita expenditure, there is no evidence of widows being disproportionately concentrated in poor households or of female-headed households being poorer than male-headed households. These findings also apply in terms of adult-equivalent consumption for any reasonable choice of equivalence scales. Poverty indices for different household types, however, are quite sensitive to the level of economies of scale. Even relatively small economies of scale imply the incidence of poverty among single widows, widows living with unmarried children, and female household heads (all of whom tend to live in relatively small households).

The disabled are no better off, since we, as a country, have failed to create a disabled-friendly society. Nor have we ensured that the disabled are able to avail the economic opportunities available to the able-bodied. Disabled people have to struggle to get admission in schools or other educational institutions that do not have seats reserved for them. Public spaces, especially roads and transportation systems, are not designed to be disabled friendly, which makes it hard for them to access economic opportunities. As a result, many of them are left with no choice but to end up begging in cities.

Finally, in the changing globalized world, families are increasingly becoming nuclear, even among the poorer sections of society. In cities, children choose to settle down independently of their parents. In rural areas, children often migrate to cities or elsewhere in search of work or better opportunities, often leaving their aged parents behind, who are then left to fend for themselves. According to studies, the population of elderly (above 60 years) in India was only 104 million in 2011 (around 10% of the population). By 2020, the median age in India will be 29 years and it will become the youngest county in the world. Hence, there is great emphasis on capitalizing the 'demographic dividend'. The number of elderly, however, is estimated to rise to 143 million by 2021, 173 million by 2026 and 324 million by 2050. Therefore, studies find that in two decades, we will surpass China in the number of elderly. Recent studies by HelpAge India finds that the condition of the elderly is worsening every year. They find that nearly four in every five of the elderly face abuse, mostly at the hands of family members. At the same time, community support systems are falling apart. With no retirement benefits, those engaged in the informal sector work till their bodies allow them to and feed themselves till they are able to. (HelpAge India, 2014a, 2014b; UNFPA, 2012)

In this context, the National Social Assistance Programme (NSAP) assumes massive importance as it is the only national level policy to provide income support to these highly vulnerable groups of people, many of whom would otherwise be on the brink of starvation and destitution. The programme was initiated in 1995 by the government to provide income support to vulnerable sections of the population. In 2009, it was expanded to include disabled and widows (PIB, 2009). However, the amount of pension remains extremely meagre. The central contribution to the scheme has remained unchanged at Rs. 200 per beneficiary (for those below 80 years) since 2006. Most states contribute some amount to add to the total received by the beneficiary. The states' contributions vary from nothing in states such as Bihar to Rs. 2000 in states in such as Goa. In most cases, the total amounts vary from Rs. 100 to Rs. 1000 (such as Delhi).

Despite the meagre amounts, studies have shown that the pensions play a major role in improving the lives of the poor. They not only make them more independent but also help them get greater respect within the household. The meagre pension amounts enable vulnerable populations to meet some of their basic expenses on items such as medicines, transport, food, support items such as crutches, glasses, etc. (Chopra and Pudussery, 2014; Gupta, 2013).

Yet, clearly the pensions amounts are hardly sufficient. Gupta (2013) did an interesting exercise where he attempted to find out the income gap of pensioners, i.e., the gap between required expenditure and incomes (excluding pensions). This gap was an indicator of the basic minimum amount that should be given as pension to these households. The average gap was around Rs. 730 in Jharkhand (where pension amount was only Rs. 400) and Rs. 700 in Chhattisgarh (where pension amount was only Rs. 300). Hence, the pensions were not enough to meet the basic needs of the destitute population. The shortfall meant the destitute people had to forgo some of their requirements. The paper also shows how pension contributions of the central government have remained constant (in real terms) between 1995 (when the program was launched) and 2011 (when the survey was conducted). Given that the amounts have not risen since 2011 and inflation has remained high, we can safely say that pension amounts (in real terms) would be lower now (in 2015) than they were two decades ago (in 1995) at the program's inception (when the central share was just Rs. 75).

The Demand for Pension by Pune's Waste Pickers

The Kagad Kach Patra Kashtakari Panchayat (KKPKP), a union of informal waste pickers in Pune, Maharashtra, conducted several rounds of studies among its workers to assess their needs and demands. As most waste pickers in Pune are women, the union is also composed primarily of women. During these discussions, old age support emerged as one of the most important and pervasive needs of informal waste pickers. The women spoke of how their formalized counterparts—sweepers and cleaners with government jobs—had income security during their old age but they did not, and how they feared what would happen during their old age as they were unsure whether their children would support them or not. They clearly stated that 'times have changed'. Children don't want to support their parents anymore. They grow up and have their own family and settle down separately. Then if you ask them to support you, they will say, 'We are unable to support our own wives and children properly. How can we also try to support you?' Besides, there are several workers without sons, and whose daughters, married off and living with in-laws, are unable to support their parents. Further, several women also stated that their sons, though living with them, are addicted to alcohol and hence, unable support even themselves.

Seeing the massive need and demand for income support among the vulnerable informal workers, KKPKP decided to assist its needy and deserving members in obtaining pensions under the Government of India's National Social Assistance Programme, to help them meet at least some of their needs.

Their efforts began around midway through 2011, when needy women were identified and their documents collected for applications.

This chapter deals with the findings that emerged over the following years during which the union tried to obtain pensions for the needy and deserving waste-picking women in Pune.

Effectiveness of Pensions in Rural Areas—Findings from the PEEP Survey

The findings of this chapter have been enriched from a second source of information as well. A study was conducted by the Indian Institute of Technology (IIT), Delhi, whereby teams of volunteers travelled across 10 states to study social protection programs in the country. The study was called the Public Evaluation of Entitlement Programmes (PEEP Survey). One of the teams, of which I was also a part, went to Nandurbar and Osmanabad districts in Maharashtra. One block was chosen in each district and four villages were randomly selected from within those blocks. The teams obtained pension lists for the four selected villages from the block office, which administers the national and state pension schemes. All the names on the list were then verified through actual meetings with the beneficiaries. Further, 12 randomly selected beneficiaries were chosen for detailed interviews from each panchayat.

In all, the team verified nearly 400 pensioners and interviewed nearly 96 of them. This exercise and our experiences also inform the content of this chapter. The study will therefore be able to draw a contrast between the implementation of the program in rural and urban areas (as it was realized that the implementation of the program varies massively between urban and rural areas).

Findings from Maharashtra Regarding Implementation of National and State Pension Schemes

After over a year of efforts and attempts, KKPKP realized that obtaining pensions for the needy was a hugely daunting task, given the complicated procedures, confusion over the requirements, and the overwhelming paperwork. This has led to the denial of pensions to several needy and deserving poor. Further, it has resulted in the extremely low reach of pensions among the urban poor and low utilization of allocated budgets.

Quite a few studies have drawn attention towards the poor design and delivery mechanism of the NSAP which often lead to exclusion of the most needy populations (Chopra and Pudussery, 2014; Gupta, 2013; TISS and Pension Parishad, 2015). Chopra and Pudussery (2014) use data from the PEEP survey in 2013 across 10 states to study the performance and issues associated with pension schemes under NSAP. Gupta (2013) uses data from a survey of 60 pension beneficiaries in Jharkhand and Chhattisgarh to study the performance, impact and issues associated with the scheme. All these studies highlight the massive procedural complications and uncertainties associated with the process of application and receipt of pensions under the NSAP.

In fact, during the hearing of a public interest litigation in the Supreme Court of India, the court also recognized the massive problems faced in implementation of the case (SC Commissioners, 2011). Pellissery (2005) presents a wonderfully detailed description of the pension application and approval mechanism and the struggles of the applicants and beneficiaries. All these studies are located in rural areas. The implementation mechanisms and experiences of applicants in urban areas are very different from their rural counterparts. This study, drawing from the experiences of urban waste pickers in Pune as well as rural poor in Nandurbar and Osmanabad, is able to present the lesser known picture of NSAP in urban Maharasthra and compare this with the situation in rural Maharashtra.

Some of the problems with the design and delivery of the pension schemes have been outlined below.

Co-existence of central and state sponsored pension schemes: The coexistence of state and centrally sponsored schemes, and the onus of their implementation resting on the same agency, leads to a great deal of confusion among not only the beneficiaries, but also among officials, about the eligibility criterion, application procedures, documentary requirements and the benefits under each.

For instance, in Maharashtra, NSAP is implemented by the Sanjay Gandhi Yojana office, which also implements the state pension scheme, i.e., the Sanjay Gandhi Niradhar Yojana (SGNY). However, while trying to apply for benefits under NSAP and SGNY in Pune, KKPKP found that the officials of the Sanjay Gandhi Yojana themselves were extremely uncertain about the differences in application procedures, eligibility criterion and requirements of both schemes. Yet, there were massive differences in eligibility criteria, application procedures and documentary requirements for each scheme. In fact, the SGNY can be said to expand the scope of pensions to include the destitute who are not covered under the NSAP.

The NSAP includes four sub-schemes, i.e.,

i. Indira Gandhi National Old Age Pension Scheme, (IGNOAPS) which provides an income of Rs. 600 per month (central share Rs. 200 and state share Rs. 400) to citizens above 65 years of age whose names are on the BPL list of the tehsil/district.
ii. Indira Gandhi National Disability Pension Scheme (IGNDPS) was started in 2009 (PIB, 2009) and provides Rs. 600 per month (central share Rs. 200 and state share Rs. 400) to persons between 18–65 years of age, with severe disabilities (above 80%), whose names are on the BPL list.
iii. Indira Gandhi National Widow Pension Scheme (IGNWPS) was started in 2009 (PIB, 2009) and provides Rs. 600 per month (central share Rs. 200 and state share Rs. 400) to women between 40–65 years of age whose husbands have passed away and whose names are on the BPL list.
iv. Indira Gandhi National Family Benefit Scheme (IGNFBS), which provides a Rs. 10,000 support to families whose names are on the BPL list and whose sole bread earners have passed away in an accident.

On the other hand, the SGNY covers people suffering from various kinds of destitution. These include devdasis, destitutes, widows, those who are divorced but not receiving any alimony or support, victims of domestic violence, women liberated from prostitution, families of agricultural workers who have committed suicide and their family income is less than Rs. 21,000, orphaned children who are less than 18 years old, and rape victims. It covers those suffering from various disabilities such as blindness, speech impairment, deafness, mental disorders, etc., and those suffering from diseases like T.B., HIV AIDS and leprosy. The conditions for receiving benefits, however, are different from the conditions under NSAP. In order to receive benefits under SGNY, the destitute must be a resident of Maharasthra for at least 15 years, must not have a son who is 25 years of age or older, and must earn an income of less than Rs. 21,000.

If anything, there was slightly greater awareness about the requirements for SGNY but none about NSAP. As a result, officials would often ask applicants to produce a combined set of documents required for each scheme.

The state scheme (SGNY) application required domicile certificates stating that the applicant had resided in the state for at least 15 years, an income certificate to prove an income lower than Rs 21,000, as well as proofs of identity, residence, age and disability (more than 40%), widowhood, illness, orphanhood (as the case may be). To apply under the national scheme, NSAP, the applicant's name was supposed to be on the district BPL list. There was no need for income certificates or domicile certificates. Yet, the officials would demand these documents.

Further, officials were often unable to even give out the appropriate application forms. When asked for application forms, they would either say they didn't have them or even if they did, they would give out application forms for SGNY.

This confusion not only leads to a great deal of harassment of the applicants, but also deprives a large section of the vulnerable poor from accessing pensions because they are neither able to understand the requirements in the first place nor obtain the plethora of documents required.

Elaborate documentary requirements that are impossible for the urban poor to produce: Even without the confusion between the central and state schemes, there is a host of paperwork that goes into pension applications, which many, particularly the truly vulnerable urban poor, are never able to produce. For instance, the NSAP requires that the applicants' names be on the panchayat (or Urban Local Bodies') BPL list, prepared according to the 2006 BPL census. However, it is well known that there are immense flaws in the census and massive inclusion and exclusion errors in the BPL lists prepared using the census.

Further, the data is extremely outdated. In several cases, it was found that households had actually slipped into poverty due to a shock which occurred after the BPL census. For instance, even if a household is well above poverty line at the time of the BPL census, the death of the male earning member and consequent restrictions on the female members' mobility and occupational choices may well pull the family into poverty. Similarly, a family may have been above poverty line in 2002, but with old age and the consequent inability to do hard manual labor, high medical expenses, and lack of working children or unwillingness of children to support old parents, may well pull the previously APL household into destitution.

The state pension scheme, Sanjay Gandhi Niradhar Yojana (SGNY), which does not require applicants to have their names on the BPL list, therefore, acts as complementary to the NSAP. It provides a ray of hope to all those destitute and vulnerable poor who are not on the state's BPL list.

The state pension scheme does, however, require proof of being poor. The applicant needs to produce an income certificate proving a household income below Rs. 21,000. The applicant must not have an able-bodied son above the age of 25 who can earn and support his parents. Finally, the scheme also requires a domicile certificate stating that the applicant has been residing in the state for the past 15 years. The applicant has to produce proof of residence in the state dating back 15 years, such as electricity bills, phone bills, house tax receipts, etc. For those who have migrated from villages, those who are homeless or those who live in informal settlements such as unrecognized slums, such documents are impossible to produce. Nothing else is treated as proof of residence (for instance, in Pune, a widow who had her husband's death certificate from 1994—with a Pune Government Hospital address—could not use that as address proof). This requirement, therefore, acts as an exclusionary criterion for the truly desperate and vulnerable urban poor population who are sure to be excluded from the purview of both the central as well as state pension programs.

Problems in obtaining the necessary documents: The lack of clarity about procedures and documentary requirements, and the impossibility of obtaining those documents for some sections of the population are not the only hurdles which the vulnerable poor have to overcome to finally avail of pensions under the state or central schemes. Obtaining each of those documents requires waiting for innumerable hours in queues in order to get stamps or signatures of various officers sitting in different offices—in the case of Pune, it even requires running to different parts of the city to visit these officers.

For instance, to obtain an income certificate one needs to go to the collector's office where one needs to stand in three different queues to finally get an affidavit stating the family income and the purpose for which the affidavit is required.

Given that one spends at least half an hour in a queue to finally reach the official sitting behind the counter, and that there are at least 30 people standing behind a person in the queue, there is no scope to argue or fight if the official asks for a certain amount of money and does not offer a receipt in return.

One then has to run to the Talathi's (revenue officer) office to get this document verified. Once again, given the rush at the Talathi's office, any amount may have to be paid to get his signature. The tired and confused applicant is unaware and/or afraid to ask for a receipt for the money, lest the Talathi deny the all important stamp and signature, and all efforts go in vain.

With the verified documents in hand, the applicant has to rush back to the collector's office where the affidavit, with the Talathi's stamp and signature, and photocopies of the relevant documents (proofs of address, identity, etc.) are submitted. The applicant then waits for the income certificate. The whole process generally takes several days and hence, can lead to several days of harassment and loss of income. For several informal sector workers, a loss of a day's income leads to inability to cook or eat food that day.

There is a similar procedure for obtaining a domicile certificate. Add a visit to the doctor at the government hospital for an age certificate (for old age pension applicants) or for a disability certificate (for disability certificate applicants).

At each of these stages, there is much greater probability of the work getting done if one pays an additional amount. One is more likely to get a disability certificate stating that the disability is greater than 40% (in case of SGNY applicants) and greater than 80% (for Indira Gandhi National Disability Pension Scheme (IGNDPS) applicants) if the doctor knows he is getting some returns for the *favor*. While the problem is less severe for urban poor with access to good quality public hospitals (as waste pickers in Pune are), it is of great significance to the rural population.

At each of the offices, whether the collector's or the Talathi's office, there are hoards of agents (middlemen) who crowd around anyone entering the building premises, promising to get the work done in a simpler and hassle-free way. The poor applicant faces a clear choice—either pay the middlemen, who know how to get what you want (because of personal/political connections or simply because he can pay the officials) or face the uncertainty of being turned away after standing in queue for hours because of a missing document, an inappropriate photograph, a missing proof of residence or simply because it is lunch time.

It is for this reason that in the villages surveyed during the PEEP survey in Maharashtra, nearly all beneficiaries of the state or national pension schemes claimed that they had paid bribes worth Rs. 400–1,500 to get their pensions started. The bribes were normally paid to an agent within the village or from a nearby village, who would help them through the application process and share the amount with officials through the chain— the Talathi, the Panchayat Secretary and the officials at the Sanjay Gandhi Yojana office who accepted the applications. For those who were unable to pay, pensions were a distant dream, irrespective of their level of destitution. However, in some (though very rare) cases, pensioners did mention that they managed without having to pay bribes because they were assisted by some politically important people in the village (see Pellissery (2005) for a graphic account of the pension approval process and an analysis of factors that work to ensure approval of a person's pension applications).

While it is desirable to have a system in place for identifying the poor and needy who do not figure on the BPL list, it is also worth questioning the basis according to which people are issued certificates that say that their income is less than Rs. 21,000. Clearly, the amount is extremely low and somewhat arbitrary— being the same for rural as well as urban areas. In a state where the monthly per capita income for BPL households is Rs. 960, even a three-member household would require an income of Rs. 34,560 to be called BPL! Then where does the magic figure of Rs. 21,000 come from?

It is also worth questioning the procedures for verifying income. In Maharashtra, the responsibility falls on the Talathi, who is supposed to visit each claimant and verify her/his claims. In certain villages this may well be possible, where communities are close knit and where people know each other. The process in rural areas is straightforward. The Talathi is supposed to look at the land records and find out the amount of land owned by the applicant. He is then supposed to estimate the annual income from the land.

However, in urban areas, where sources of income can be very diverse (and not dependent upon the amount of physical assets such as land), it seems improbable that one person can visit claimants from all the formal/informal slums and verify their claims. And even if the Talathi manages to visit the claimants, what tools does he have to verify their claims regarding their annual income? Will he look at their household assets or the number of able-bodied members in the household? In the end, the decision to award the certificate would be largely based on the Talathi's discretion. With discretionary powers comes the power to demand bribes. Ultimately, as Pellissery, (2005) notes, the decision to award pensions is completely arbitrary and based on the discretion of the officials sitting to accept applications, and the chairperson and members of the committee, which sits to decide upon the fate of the applications.

Irregularity in pension payments: Even once the pensions are approved, the disbursements take place highly irregularly. In both the districts surveyed, the receipt of pensions was found to be highly erratic. The PEEP survey was conducted in June 2013. However, in Nandurbar district, all NSAP beneficiaries who were surveyed had last received the state government's contribution towards their pensions in November 2012, and the central government's contribution in February 2013. Similar findings have come from studies in other states as well (Chopra and Pudussery, 2014; Gupta, 2013; HelpAge India, 2014b; MoRD, 2013; TISS and Pension Parishad, 2015). TISS and Pension Parishad (2015) finds that the erratic nature of pension payments is because they are 'bunched up'. In other words, districts release payments for several months at a time. However, the reasons for pension payments being bunched up are not very clear. Discussions with officials at the Sanjay Gandhi Yojana office in Pune revealed that pension payments were bunched up on purpose to reduce official work. They claimed that each time pension money had to paid, they would have to physically go to the different banks where beneficiaries held accounts. At the banks, they would have to submit the list of beneficiaries with accounts in the bank, along with cheques for corresponding pension payments. Given the huge work load, this was not possible for them to do every month, hence they preferred to bunch up payments for several months at a time. However, TISS and Pension Parishad (2015) find that the bunching up of pension payments happen 'due to the delay in the funds being transferred from the state treasury involving long and bureaucratic procedures'. Yet, as all studies find, though the pension of several months is received together, they generally receive the entire amount.

However, as all studies report, the erratic nature of payments causes immense problems for the beneficiaries. First, not knowing when the next payment might come, they are unable to plan their expenses so as to last them till the next payments come.

Second, in the absence of any system for informing about arrival of pensions in their accounts, they often need to make several visits to the banks/post offices to check.

Third, due to the erratic nature of pension payments, beneficiaries are never really sure whether their payments have been siphoned, suspended, stopped or simply delayed. As TISS and Pension Parishad (2015) report that in Kerala 'many reported being confused of the amount that was actually due to them'. 85-year-old Kooken from Edavaka panchayat, the lone elderly person (amongst the 13 people in the above-80 age group), who was availing the enhanced pension due to people above 80 years of age, received a total of Rs. 9,900 (pension for nine months) in two instalments in quick concession. Due to the lumpsum amount he received, he was under the impression that he had received his pension for the entire year.

This also creates confusion on the process of payments. In Rajasthan people interpreted this as 'their pension had stopped for four months'. This is a key administrative black hole that needs special attention. It needs to be explored further, whether this is a delay for four months, whether the pension amount for four months has not been received at the panchayat level or whether the pension has genuinely been discontinued. The inconvenience caused by lack of information and options for redressal is quite high. In some cases, pensioners need to 'reapply' for pensions. In other cases of delay, they reapply in any case leading to administrative confusion.

Lack of awareness of pension amounts: In Nandurbar and Osmanabad districts, the survey of pensioners included questions on the level of awareness regarding their entitled monthly pension amounts. Surprisingly, only about half of those receiving pensions were aware of the actual amounts they were entitled to. Most people were only able to mention the amount that they were able to withdraw from the bank, which itself was erratic, ranging from Rs. 400 to Rs. 3,000 for several months combined together. The situation in Maharashtra, however, is clearly worse than most other districts in this regard. Chopra and Pudussery (2014), using PEEP survey data in 10 states, find that awareness about pension amounts were high in most states, the highest being in Odisha and Chhattisgarh where 100% of the beneficiaries were aware of the exact amount of their pension entitlement. Other states such as Uttar Pradesh, Tamil Nadu and Rajasthan also fared well as over 90% of the beneficiaries were aware of their entitlements.

The reason for the lack of awareness regarding pensions lies in the erratic nature of pension disbursements. In Maharashtra, the erratic nature of pensions is compounded by the divergence between the state and central schemes for pension payments. Beneficiaries of pensions under NSAP receive Rs. 200 from the central government (under the IGNOAPS, IGNDPS or IGNWPS, and Rs. 500 in the case of people above 80 years of age) and Rs. 400 from the state government (under the Shravan Bal Yojana—the state government's scheme to top up the amount of pension received under the NSAP). However, the two amounts do not always come together. In fact, inspections of beneficiaries' passbooks revealed that they normally received several months of money from one or either source. For instance, when we checked their passbooks during the survey (in June, 2013), we found that beneficiaries in Osmanabad had last received Rs. 800 in February 2013. This Rs. 800 comprised four months of the central government's share of pensions. Prior to that, they had received Rs. 1,200 in November 2012, which was actually the state government's share of the pension amount for three months (August, September and October). In the face of such erratic payments, it becomes very difficult or even impossible for beneficiaries (or anyone else) to track whether they have received their full amounts, what they are yet to receive and when they can expect to receive it. The only yardstick for comparison, therefore, is other beneficiaries in the community. Panic strikes when one realises that they have not received their pensions even as others in the community have. Does this mean their pensions have stopped? Should they then go and enquire whether their names have been removed from the list, as often happens with beneficiaries?

Lack of proper (detailed) entries in bank passbooks: During the survey in Nandurbar and Osmanabad, the survey team also tried to verify whether the pensioners were receiving their entitled pension amounts by studying their bank passbooks. However, the surveyors soon realized that this was not an easy task given the lack of details mentioned in the passbooks. Most of the pensioners had accounts in cooperative banks, which issued passbooks with hand-written entries, with no details of the sources of credit into the account. However, several pensioners had accounts with nationalized banks such as State Bank of India, Maharashtra Gramin Bank and Bank of Maharashtra, in which the passbook entries were computerized. However, even these banks did not enter the full details of the credits made to the pensioners' accounts. For instance, they did not mention the months for which the amounts had been credited. Some of them did not even mention the scheme under which the amounts had been credited (for instance, the central government component or the state government component). This made it extremely difficult, and in some cases, even impossible to assess for certain whether the pensioners had been receiving the full amount or whether some months had been skipped, and how many months of pension payments were remaining.

Determining the appropriate mode of payment is a complicated task. Gupta (2013) finds through this study in Jharkhand and Chhattisgarh that there were huge problems with payments through banks. Out of 60 beneficiaries that were surveyed, 46 actually stated that they would prefer cash payments through the panchayat rather than bank payments. It is worth noting that bank payments were introduced due to the massive irregularities, lack of transparency and accountability in payments. However, the difficulties that the poor face in accessing, understanding and utilising the banking system for their meagre pension payments leaves them desiring the old system of payments through money orders, post offices or cash payments through banks.

Many of these problems faced by pension beneficiaries in rural Maharashtra have been detailed in Pellissery (2005).

Failing co-operative banks and problems with opening accounts in nationalised banks: In Osmanabad district, the surveyors found that most pensioners received their pensions in district cooperative banks. However, none of these pensioners had received their pension payments since February 2013. When they visited the banks, they were informed that the bank did not have enough money to pay their pension amounts. On investigating further, the surveyors learnt that most of the district cooperative banks in the region had become dysfunctional, following excessive loan disbursals and non-repayment of large loan amounts by the rural elites and ruling classes. The banks had thus stopped making payments and the account holders could not even withdraw from their savings.

People thus tried to shift to nationalized banks, which are supposed to be more secure. However, several pensioners who tried to open accounts in nationalized banks reported facing extreme difficulties in getting accounts opened. Despite having submitted complete application forms along with the supporting documents, and running back and forth for over six months, the bank officials had refused to open their accounts. It is possible that given the low volume and value of transactions by pensioners, the already overburdened nationalized banks see little incentive to open accounts for receipt of pension payments.

In Pune, it was found that even waste pickers who had accounts in nationalised banks were compulsorily told to open accounts in cooperative banks (mostly in the Pune District Central Cooperative Bank Ltd.), possibly to reduce administrative workload. However, the precise reasons for this are not clear.

Several other problems exist with the scheme which cause tremendous harassment to the beneficiaries. In particular, lack of a mandatory timeline for activities creates a lot of uncertainty and harassment. Applicants are not aware of how long it would take for decisions to be taken upon their applications. Officials at the Sanjay Gandhi Yojana revealed that the pension approval committee was scheduled to meet every quarter (three months). However, meetings rarely took place every quarter and were very irregular.

Pellissery (2005) describes in graphic detail the actual process of approval of pensions and its inherent arbitrariness which then naturally leads to massive inclusion and (to a lesser extent) exclusion errors. It is hard to imagine how the arbitrary nature of the beneficiary selection process can be rectified without strong local participatory and community institutions such as gram sabha (in villages) and mohalla sabha/ward sabha (in cities). In the absence of these institutions, universalization appears to be a necessary step to ensure the truly needy are not excluded from the scheme.

Finally the absence of a dedicated grievance redressal mechanism implies that in case of grievances, the applicants/beneficiaries have to turn to the same set of people who might be involved in causing the grievance in the first place. Thus, when a pension application is rejected without providing any satisfactory reason, or a pension that has been granted is suddenly stopped due to personal rivalry or simply to favor another applicant, there is no one to address the concerns of the aggrieved claimant.

THE BRIGHT SIDE

The survey did, however, also find a few very positive and encouraging signs in the functioning of the pension schemes.

Very few people on the pension list who could not be found or who had died more than six months earlier: The PEEP survey involved a social audit whereby the list of pension beneficiaries was obtained from the Sanjay Gandhi Yojana office at the block headquarters. The surveyors then visited each person on the list and asked them whether they were receiving their entitled pension amounts. The audit revealed that there were very few people on the lists who could not be traced (where the villagers had not heard of their names) or who had died more than six months earlier (i.e., someone else was possibly accessing pensions in the name of dead people). The verification exercise helped refute claims that pension amounts are sanctioned and disbursed for 'ghost' pensioners and are actually appropriated by others.

Good coverage in villages: The survey also found that the national and state pension schemes together managed a fairly good coverage in rural areas with a large proportion of the elderly, disabled and widowed actually receiving their pensions.

Very useful for those receiving a pension: Finally, the survey also asked detailed questions about the utility and importance of the pension amounts among the beneficiaries. It found that the pension, though extremely meager, erratic and unreliable, was still extremely helpful for those who received it. Several elderly men and women described how it made it possible for them to lead an independent life—they did not need have to ask anyone for money for tea and medicines.

The Way Forward

Given the above discussion on the findings about the implementation of the pension programmes, the way forward is clear.

Increased awareness and clarity regarding the differences in eligibility criteria, requirements and benefits from the state and the central schemes: We have described above the confusion regarding the differences between state and central pension schemes. The confusion exists not only amongst the deserving elderly and destitutes, but also among officials administering them. This leads to a great deal of harassment of those trying to access the pensions, as they are asked to fulfill the requirements of both the schemes. Therefore, increased awareness and clarity regarding each aspect of these schemes would be extremely helpful in reducing harassment and helping deserving elderly and destitute access the benefits of the schemes.

Reducing documentary requirements: This is probably the most difficult suggestion to implement because each of the required documents is essential to prove that the person meets the eligibility criteria. However, the greater the documentary requirement, the greater is the cost (time and money) for the applicant, and greater is the probability of exclusion of the most vulnerable.

The more targeted the scheme, the greater will be the requirement of documents. There is, therefore, a strong case for a move towards the universalization of pensions, such that any proof of identity would be sufficient for availing of pension benefits. The more universalized and less targeted the scheme, the lesser will be the requirement for documents to prove the applicant's eligibility. For instance, if having sons above a certain age group is not a criteria for declining pensions, there would no longer be a need for producing ration cards. Since ration cards are often difficult to obtain for rural migrants in urban areas, this would lead to the inclusion of a large number of migrants. Further, if income is no longer a criterion for availing pensions, there would be no need to produce income certificates or documents to prove that one's name is on the BPL list.

Simplifying procedures for applications and availing of essential documents: The government of Rajasthan has taken revolutionary steps to facilitate availing of documents, filing pension applications and enrolling beneficiaries, following the passage of the state government's orders regarding universalization of social security pensions on 1 April 2013. The entire administration has been involved in holding camps and assisting people in obtaining necessary documents and filing pension applications. While the camps have managed to greatly simplify procedures and enroll a number of beneficiaries, it is not clear whether sustainable long-term systems could be set up for this. Moreover, the Rajasthan pension schemes have been criticized for huge inclusion errors, as the simple procedures and the stress on inclusion have allowed several well-off households to avail of social security pensions meant for the poor. However, this problem can largely be attributed to faults in the system of identification of the poor rather than being specific to the identification of pension beneficiaries.

An improvement in the system for availing necessary documents such as voter IDs, income certificates, ration cards and domicile certificates is urgently required in most parts of the country. Such an improvement would have far-reaching impacts on the lives of people. Specifically, the system needs to be designed to be better geared towards the needs of migrants. With migrants constituting over 30% of the country's population, it is strange that the system is still not prepared to deal with migrants and their requirements.

Finally, it has been stated often that one of the most effective ways to reduce inclusion errors is to make the scheme more inclusive. In fact, it has been found time and again, that identification of the rich or 'who is to be excluded' is often much easier than identifying the poor, i.e., those to be included. Therefore, a good way to make pensions inclusive of the truly vulnerable would be to simply include applicants by default, unless there is evidence of their belonging to the excluded category—for instance, those paying income taxes, those who own motorized vehicles or more than a certain amount of land, etc.

Regularizing pension payments: Given that several districts still follow manual systems of transferring money to the beneficiaries, the task of depositing money every month may be unfeasible for some government departments. However, in such cases, the departments may do well to self-assess their own capacity and figure out how often and how regularly they are able to deposit money in all accounts. Having some sort of known payment schedule, even if the payments are not monthly, allows the pensioners to plan their expenditures accordingly.

Improving the spread, reach and capacity of banking systems: Given the increasing number of social sector services being rendered by public sector banks and the urgency of those services for the nation's poor, it may make sense to undertake a massive campaign to increase the spread, reach and capacity of the banking system to respond to the exponential rise in demand for banking services among the poor.

Mandatory computerization of passbook updating systems and disclosure of all details of transactions: Given that passbooks, in most cases, have become the sole documentary evidence of social security services reaching the poor, it is important that passbook updating systems themselves be updated. A manually updated passbook with entries written in illegible handwriting and with no details of the transaction mentioned whatsoever, leaves people with no evidence or record of the receipt of their pensions for all practical purposes. On the other hand, a regularly updated passbook, with computerized entries and details of all entries mentioned, such as date of credit, source of credit, name of scheme under which the amount was credited and the month for which the amount was credited, greatly facilitates verification and awareness generation among the beneficiaries.

Finally, it is worth mentioning that the demand for pensions for vulnerable populations has taken on a national unified character under the banner of the 'pension parishad', i.e., a coalition of organisations, unions, activists, academics, artists and a variety of people affected or moved by the condition of vulnerable people in India. The movement, which has held several large demonstrations in various parts of the country, has been campaigning with the state and central level political class since 2012 for a basic set of demands.

Pension Parishad Demands

- A Universal and Non Contributory Old Age Pension System to be established immediately by the government with a minimum amount of m onthly pension not less than 50% of minimum wage or Rs. 2,000 per month, whichever is higher.
- The pension to be an individual entitlement for all eligible citizens of India.
- The monthly pension amount to be indexed to inflation bi-annually and revised every two to three years in the same manner as is done for salaries/pensions of government servants.
- Any individual who is 55 years or older to be eligible for the old age pension.
- For women, eligibility age for pensions to be 50 years.
- For highly vulnerable groups (such as the Primitive Tribal Groups, Transgender, Sex Workers, PWDs), the eligibility age to be 45 years or fixed according to their particular circumstances.
- No one to be forced to compulsorily retire from work on attaining the age of eligibility for universal old age pension.
- A single window system for Old Age Pensions.
- APL/BPL criteria should not be used for exclusion.
- The payment of pension not to be used to deny any other social security/welfare benefit such as benefit under the Public Distribution System.

Exclusion Criteria

- Individuals whose income is higher than the threshold level for payment of income tax
- Individuals who are receiving pension from any other sources that exceeds the pension amount under the Universal Old Age Pension Programme.

(as mentioned on the official website of the pension parishad www.pensionparishad.org)

Conclusion

Ramakumar (undated) describes how funds for pensions are allocated in a way that assumes that only half the eligible beneficiaries would avail pensions under NSAP. Therefore, if a larger number of eligible claimants apply, pensions would have to be rationed—some eligible beneficiaries would be provided while others would not. How does the system select the successful applicants? Pellissery (2005) wonderfully illustrates the process of application and selection of beneficiaries through a study of rural Maharashtra. He clearly illustrates how the existence of a 'limit' on the number of beneficiaries (which is less than the actual number of eligible people) feeds a system of political clientalism. Local political elites exert and expand their influence upon the poor claimants through their power to influence success of pension applications and continuance of pensions.

Given this scenario, the demands of the pension parishad, particularly of universalisation of pensions, appear extremely relevant to ensure that the poor and needy do not get left out.

It is also worth mentioning that several of the problems, which have been described here have been recognized not only in earlier studies but also by the government. It is in recognition of these problems and as a response to the demands of the Pension Parishad that the Ministry of Rural Development set up a task force to review the NSAP and make recommendations for its reform. The task force echoed several of the problems and demands highlighted by the Pension Parishad (MoRD, 2013). Following this, the Ministry of Rural Development published revised guidelines for implementation of the NSAP (MoRD, 2014). The revised guidelines again took a step towards simplication of procedures and expansion of the pensions but fell dramatically short of the demands of the Pension Parishad and the need of the hour. The revised guidelines do not fix responsibilities in case of delays in disbursement. They do not talk about a mechanism to inform people that their pensions have been credited (if payment is timely, perhaps that won't be needed, but given that it's not timely right now), actual expansion of coverage, and indexing payments (central contribution to pensions have been Rs. 200 since 2006). Finally, while the guidelines do mention universalistion to eligible beneficiaries, that is hardly a solace. Given the strict eligibility conditions (particularly related to the person's name being on the BPL list), both exclusion and inclusion errors are likely to remain rampant and the needy are likely to remain excluded from their right.

Finally, it is also not clear whether and when the revised guidelines even would actually be implemented. The Supreme Court hearing the right to food case (People's Union for Civil Liberties vs. Union of India (civil writ petition 196 of 2001)) had, in 2011, given several interim orders related to efficient functioning of the NSAP. These include the following:

- State governments shall complete the identification of persons entitled for a pension under the NOAPS, and ensure that it is paid regularly.
- Payment of the pension under the scheme shall be made before seventh day of each month.
- The scheme shall not be discontinued without any preceding order from the Supreme Court.

* The NOAPS grants paid by the central government to the state governments under 'additional central assistance' shall not be diverted for any other purposes. These orders in the right to food case are 'judiciable', and they have given an impetus to local movements, while also creating a monitoring system through 'food commissioners' and state-level advisors to the commissioners. (Gupta, 2013)

Yet, besides one of these orders (that the scheme shall not be discontinued), most states have not complied with the Supreme Court's orders. Pension payments continue to be erratic. No state makes payments by the seventh of each month. Even in Odisha, the best performing state according the PEEP survey (Chopra and Pudussery, 2014) pension payments are made on the 15th of each month, although they are made regularly. It is worth exploring why governments are resistant to abide by the recommendations of their own commissions or of the Supreme Court, and what sort of pressure may help to turn the political tables.

References

Chopra, S., and Pudussery, J. (2014), 'Social security pensions in India— An assessment', *Economic and Political Weekly*, XLIX(19), 68–74.

Dreze, J., and Srinivasan, P. V. (1997), 'Widowhood and poverty in rural India: Some inferences from household survey data', *Journal of Development Economics*, 54(2), 217–234.

Gupta, A. (2013), 'Old Age Pension Scheme in Jharkhand and Chhattisgarh', *Economic and Political Weekly*, XLVIII(34), 54–59.

HelpAge India (2014a), *Elder Abuse in India, 2014*, New Delhi: HelpAge India.

HelpAge India (2014b), *State of India's Elderly, 2014*, HelpAge India.

MoRD (2013), *Proposal for Comprehensive National Social Assistance Programme—Report of the Task Force*, New Delhi: Ministry of Rural Development, Government of India. Retrieved from http://nsap.nic.in/nsap/Report_Task_Force_Comprehensive_NSAP.pdf

MoRD (2014), *National Social Assistance Programme—Programme Guidelines*, Ministry of Rural Development, Government of India. Retrieved from http://nsap.nic.in/Guidelines/nsap_guidelines_oct2014.pdf

Pellissery, S. (2005), 'Process deficits or political constraints? Bottom-up evaluation of non-contributory social protection policy for rural labourers in India', *Chronic Poverty Research Centre Working Paper*, (54). Retrieved from http://papers.ssrn.com/sol3/papers.cfm?abstract_id=1753683

PIB, M. (2009, February 19), Expansion of National Social Assistance Programme (NSAP)to include other vulnerable groups of the society. Press Information Bureau, Government of India. Retrieved from http://www.pib.nic.in/newsite/erelease.aspx?relid=47687

Ramakumar, R., Financing of old age pensions in Maharashtra: A note. Unpublished.

TISS, and Pension Parishad (2015), 'Summary Report of 8 State Study on Implementation of National Social Assistance Programme' (Unpublished Report), Mumbai: Tata Institute of Social Sciences, Mumbai, and Pension Parishad.

UNFPA (2012), *Report on the Status of Elderly in Select States of India, 2011* (201), New Delhi: United Nations Population Fund. Retrieved from http://www.isec.ac.in/AgeingReport_28Nov2012_LowRes-1.pdf

Our Secure Beliefs and their Insecure Lives

Sex workers organize for change

SHUBHA CHACKO, GOWRI VIJAYAKUMAR AND
SUBADRA PANCHANADESWARAN

INTRODUCTION

Sex workers' access to social security hinges on their relationship to the state. Are sex workers criminals, victims, vectors of disease, or ordinary citizens? Often, sex workers have occupied multiple positions at once. Since the colonial period in India, legal reforms and public health initiatives have sought to contain, categorize, and criminalize sex work. Sex work regulation was often linked to British anxieties about race, femininity and miscegenation (Levine, 2003; Tambe, 2009), and later to nationalist reformers' vision for a free, modern India (Nair, 1994; Vijaisri, 2005). In the 1970s and 1980s, sex workers encountered the state in a new way: in relation to the threat of the AIDS epidemic and sex workers' new access to a growing transnational sex workers' movement. Today, the state's contradictory relationship to sex work plays a central role in sex workers' insecurity. While sex work is not technically illegal in India, existing legislation pertaining to sex workers defines prostitution as sexual exploitation and criminalizes many aspects of sex work. These laws have concrete everyday effects. Police harassment is a defining feature of sex workers' working lives.

The state indulges in 'doublespeak' vis-à-vis sex workers. One arm of the state (National Aids Control Organisation) is designing interventions to encourage sex workers to use condoms or access screening services (both significantly associated with a history of sexually-transmitted infections). Some other arms (the police and the courts, for example) work hard to hunt, penalize and punish sex workers (WHO, 2005). Yet others (Department of Women and Child Development, and the National Commission of Women) are involved in rescue and rehabilitation.

While the representation of sex workers as dancers and singers is the stuff of some of the popular pathos-filled movies, the image of the sex workers remains one of a woman out to make 'quick money' or as a 'passive victim' who took a wrong turn and is now mired in a world of sleaze. Male and transgender are almost entirely absent in popular media. Female, male and transgender sex workers can come from all walks of life, but in India (as in most developing countries), they are more likely to come from poor and marginalized communities that have historically faced significant discrimination and stigma. The added stigma associated with selling sex, 'the whore stigma,' (Pheterson, 1993) and the fact that their activities are largely criminalized greatly accentuates their vulnerability. While the public health system in the country leaves much to be desired and higher fees for services at private clinics prevent the use of private sexual health services, sex workers (along with some of the other discriminated-against groups) face a host of additional challenges. For transgender sex workers, the lack of recognition of their choice of gender further complicates issues.

Sex workers as a group have been invisible and hypervisible simultaneously. While most policy documents and general literature on work, gender, etc., fail to mention sex workers rendering them invisible, in the public sphere they are hypervisible as 'bad and immoral women—visible to arms of the state that seek to punish them and invisible to others. As a group these also lack social power in such fundamental ways that they have remained voiceless for hundreds of years and excluded from society, polity and economy in myriad ways. In the last decade, several sex workers' advocacy groups have emerged both across India and around the word. Their emergence in the public arena, driven by HIV-centered activism and their self-organization into collectives, has enabled them to make their lives visible and work against their age-old legal and social marginalization.

Viewing Sex Work as Work: Unexceptional and Part of the Informal Sector

Internationally, debates about sex work have often been polarized between an approach that sees sex work as 'oppression' and one that focuses on 'empowerment' (Weitzer, 2007). In response to this polarized choice vs. coercion debate, recent scholarship (Agustin, 2007; Kotiswaran, 2010; Boris, Gilmore and Parrenas, 2011) as well as activism have suggested that a perspective that envisions sex work within a labor perspective is the best way out.

The debates around sex work and its legal status in India have also been polarized (George, Vindhya and Ray, 2010). However, the debates have been slightly different in India: unlike sex worker activists in the North, who often celebrate sex positivity and women's freedom of sexual choice, sex worker activists in India have been more likely to position themselves as poor and marginal workers. For example, Shah (2003) suggests placing sex work more squarely within the context of poverty, migration and broader shifts toward informalization in labor regimes globally.

These formulations of sex work de-exceptionalize sex work, insisting that sex work resembles other kinds of gendered informal work. Scholars in India (Sahni, 2012) also argue that such an approach is a better representation of the ways in which sex workers often describe what they do—as labor comparable to other forms of informal sector labor. It may be useful to conceptualise sex work as the active *purchase* of sexual services by clients and not necessarily the *sale* of the sex workers' body. Further, given that sex work often comprises many physical and mental activities to produce sexual labor, it may be useful to understand this from the perspective of affective labor. However, the biggest hurdle in terms of viewing sex work within the 'work' paradigm stems from the exchange of money for the provision of sexual services. While sex workers gain from receiving immediate access to cash and the flexibility that this form of work provides, they are often unable to avail of productive and profitable financial services owing to the stigma attached to sex work.

Under capitalism most work tends to be exploitive. One is either exploited or living off the exploitation of others; with most of us doing both. Under a capitalist and patriarchal system, sex (as with a range of aspects of our lives) is often commodified and used as a means of exploitation. The problem, however, is to single out sex work as exploitative. As Gothoskar and Kaiwar argue, 'unlike all other workers who sell their "labour power" sex workers are seen as "selling their bodies". This singling out has a lot more to do with perceptions rather than material realities—perceptions around sex itself'. Fighting sex work instead of fighting capitalism and patriarchy does not address the exploitation in the industry nor is it useful to the sex workers.

It must also be pointed out here that all people employed in worksites of the informal, unorganized and invisible sectors of the economy have their rights routinely violated. The more illegal or invisible the worksite, the greater its exploitative character. Criminalization of sex work leads to many human rights violations and violence—unsafe conditions, lack of healthcare services and stigmatization.

For sex workers, as it is with others in the informal economy, (re)considering them as workers is a significant conceptual and practical shift as it brings issues such as work conditions, social protection and security, voice, and participation rights to the policy table. From those in the informal sector across all identities and divides, their work and their labor, leading to their livelihood and sense of dignity, has been, we suggest, an identity of great value to them. Sex workers have been pressing for the recognition of this identity for decades, if not centuries. A strong worker identity is necessary for all of them to engage with the political economy and it can also influence the way women negotiate within the family, the community and the public sphere.

Part of the difficulty in appropriately netting female labor is because of the nature/style of women's work. It appears that the more male-like the activities of females, the more likely that it will be measured and noticed. Sex work is feminized labor (both in its content and embodiment) as are a range of occupations. Sex work offers one of the few opportunities for certain women as well as some men and transpeople to ensure survival or economic mobility. When we consider the arguments around whether sex work should be counted as work, the broader labor market conditions must be considered when we take into account a person's decision to sell sexual services. It is, without doubt, an industry that is dominated by women, with the customers being largely men.

It is, therefore, unsurprising that 'sex work' has not been recognized as a gainful activity. Not only is this an occupation that is dominated by women but it is also drenched in moralistic indignation and ideological myopia. Women in sex work therefore inhibit a shadowy underground economy where their rights as workers and citizens are routinely crushed.

The tendency to devalue and reduce the complexity of the sex workers' working lives is in keeping with the dismissal of the workers in the informal sector as unskilled (and by inference without a knowledge base). The exception being the artisan who is thought of as seeped in traditional knowledge (perceived as static). (Aneka, et al., 2013)

Legal Infrastructure

Today's laws pertaining to sex work have their roots in British India. After a newly independent India signed the International Convention for the Suppression of Traffic in Persons and of the Exploitation of the Prostitution of Others in 1950, a new version of SITA (Suppression of Immoral Traffic in Women and Girls Act) was passed in 1956. This Act was amended in 1966 and 1986, and renamed the Immoral Traffic (Prevention) Act. The amendments introduced several changes, including making the legislation gender-neutral rather than specific to women and girls.

While the UN's approach to trafficking, such as in the 2000 Protocol to Prevent, Suppress and Punish Trafficking in Persons Especially Women and Children, focusses on various forms of trafficking, ITPA, like SITA and its colonial precursors, address only trafficking for prostitution. The Act, after the 1986 amendment, defines prostitution as 'sexual exploitation or abuse of persons for commercial purposes or for consideration in money or in any other kind'. While it does not directly penalize prostitution, it penalizes various activities associated with prostitution—knowingly renting a space for use as a brothel; living on the earnings of a prostitute once over the age of 18; and inducing or procuring people to carry out prostitution. The 1986 version of ITPA also criminalizes the soliciting of clients at a distance of 200 meters from a public place. An offender can be held in a corrective institution or rehabilitation home indefinitely. The Act also allows a special police officer to conduct searches without warrants of suspected brothels, and gives the local magistrate power to order the closure of a suspected brothel and the eviction of its residents.

The Immoral Traffic (Prevention) Act (ITPA) was developed to deal with trafficking, but does not address the concerns of trafficked women. These primarily deal with the abuse of human rights including violence and exploitation by law enforcement personnel. Under the Act, selling sex as a means of livelihood is not a crime. In reality, however, the Act is often used to arrest, chargesheet, prosecute and convict women. Rescue and rehabilitation of women is the main support service envisaged by ITPA, and provided by government and non-government agencies. Trafficked women are 'rescued' and placed in approved shelter homes in order to safeguard them from abuse and exploitation. However, human rights violations such as forced medical examinations and appalling living conditions drive young girls and women back into sex work, thereby failing to reintegrate them with mainstream society.

Women are technically free to prostitute themselves for their own livelihood, while traffickers are to be penalized. However, the police arrest women rather than brothel owners because they are often bribed by the latter. Rather than protecting their rights, the police action disempowers women further because it leads to loss of income and spiraling debt that leaves them vulnerable to bondage to brothel owners/pimps/traffickers. Furthermore, the police do not inform women of the reasons for their arrest, and often extort money and/or sexually exploit them.

Profile of Sex Workers

According to National AIDS Control Organisation (NACO), there are 8.3 lakh female sex workers (FSWs) in India and about 1.1 lakh sex workers in Karnataka. A recent study by Sahini and Shankar (2011) says that about 15% of them came into sex work when they were less than 15 years old; however, the lower entry age has to be seen in the context of the informal labor market. Like in many other labor markets, women enter the profession as minors. This in fact seems to be less pronounced in sex work than in other informal labor markets (Sahini and Shankar).

Surveys conducted among sex workers in different parts of India reveal that most of them have low levels of formal education. There is an over-representation of women from the oppressed castes among sex workers, as well as of widows and women whose husbands or partners have deserted them. Often they were contending with major financial issues (debt, health issues in the family, lack of any other breadwinner) when they entered sex work.

The pan-India study (Sahini and Shankar, 2011), found that nearly 70% of the female sex workers in the country join sex work voluntarily, and were not trafficked and coerced into it. The study also revealed that about 50% of the sex workers who were surveyed have worked in different occupations and livelihood options before they entered sex work. The move was primarily due to the low incomes that they received from the work they were previously involved in. It is also found that women in sex work are a part of other labor markets. Women move to sex work from other labor markets for a variety of reasons—higher income (compared to other jobs that might be open to them), flexibility of timing and earnings, availability of cash on an immediate basis, etc.

Sex workers work in varied settings and arrangements. They are urban- and rural-based. Often they move away from their place of residence to engage in sex work. This may be to seek anonymity or to increase their chances of picking up clients or increased earnings.

For some of them sex work is the only occupation, while for others it is part-time. The part-timers combine sex work with one or more occupations. This includes engaging as daily wage laborers in construction or agricultural activities, vending, domestic work, work in garment factories, etc.

Previous studies conducted in India have used various criteria to distinguish between types of sex workers based on practice, mode of operation, mode of organization, nature of the sex work network, place of sex, and primary place of solicitation. However, often using a combination of the place of solicitation and place of sex reveals a more complex reality of sex workers. Currently sex workers work under extremely exploitative and stigmatized conditions; they are abused by police, thugs/goons, house-owners, neighbors, lodge owners, brothel owners, agents (the unpopular name being pimps) clients, husbands/partners, government officials and even strangers who see them at work. Within the system sex workers are routinely denied basic entitlements such as ration cards or access to health facilities. Their children also face discrimination in schools, hostels and in society in general. Access to public places—parks, bus stops, places of worship, restaurants, etc.—becomes unpleasant, difficult or downright traumatic. This is primarily due to societal stigmatization of their work, and by implication, of them.

Sex Workers as Legal and Social Outsiders

The fact that sex workers overwhelmingly work outside the law has implications for their health that are hard to quantify. For groups that share what Fraser describes as 'socially despised sexualities', (Fraser, 1997) cultural discrimination is accompanied by economic discrimination and isolation. The legal climate, the deep-seated 'moral' prejudice, which are overlaid with issues of gender, class and caste makes sex workers one of the more marginalized groups of people in the country.

The institutions from where they seek justice—the police, courts, informal 'panchayats' are not just uncaring but often active perpetrators of violence and other violations. Because of criminalization, sex workers are subjected to raids, rape, beating and extortion by the authorities and other non-state actors (goons, thugs, local touts, political henchmen, etc.). They often need to pay them off regularly and/or 'allow' themselves to be sexually exploited to get away from getting further victimized.

This harsh reality that they cope with everyday was succinctly expressed by a sex worker: 'When the goondas whip out a knife, we just hope to negotiate our way out of the situation. One middle-class woman from an international NGO said to us, "You must go the police." Does she not know that the police are often just goondas in uniforms? And often the two have a cozy relationship!' said one sex worker in Bangalore.

Besides atrocities faced at the hands of the police and the local thugs, self-appointed 'moral police' also unleash violence on sex workers. 'These groups call us names, chase us and tell us that they want to "clean up" the area and hence we ('the dirty women') are supposed to leave the place.'

The forced evictions from workplaces (as well as homes) and subsequent government failure to provide effective remedies drives sex workers deeper into poverty—with most of the people affected living in worse conditions than before the evictions.

Most of them do not possess ration cards or voter ID cards because they find it difficult to provide proper proof of address as their place of residence changes often. The owner of the place she resides in is not willing to give her any proof of documents as they fear trouble. Even in government departments they are not seen as 'worthy' citizens deserving of entitlements.

Sex workers also have difficulties in accessing a range of services and entitlements. A focus on health facilities is exemplar. The moment their identity is known, they face extensive systemic discrimination. Doctors as well as other health professionals hesitate to touch them assuming that they are 'carrying an infection'. Fearing these negative responses, they tend to hide the fact that they are sex workers and many of their health problems are thus left unattended. If they are living with HIV then the discrimination they face is worse. They also do not have access to non-judgmental and safe facilities for abortions during unplanned pregnancies. If an HIV+ sex worker heads to the hospital to deliver her baby, the hospital officials generally turn her away under the pretext that the kits required for the procedure are unavailable. There are inadequate support systems for sex workers when they need care. Even if they are referred through NGOs, the hospital staff are aware that they are sex workers since they know the work focus of the NGO.

Besides sex workers themselves facing violence and discrimination, their children also face discrimination from teachers (including separate seating, name calling, etc.) and students as they are considered a 'polluting' influence. Instances where wardens and teachers felt they could sexually harass or exploit the girls (daughters of sex workers) and their mothers, were also reported. The need to establish the father's name in schools also causes sex workers to be anxious about admitting their children to schools. At times mothers are forced to leave an area or village due to violence or fear of being found out and hence they are unable to go back to get the transfer certificate, etc., for their children, getting admission to a new school difficult. The criminalization of sex workers also has implications for their children. During times of raids or arrests the situation of the child can be quite horrifying. They are often subjected to gross human rights violations.

Sex workers often feel that they have no place in society; they don't expect help but they feel that they should at least be left alone to earn their living. They are in constant fear of getting caught and are often forced to perform sex work secretively. They are often exploited by brothel owners but these people are sometimes their only support and their protectors as well.

Some of them work in CBOs, but even here they are exploited to the maximum and paid very little salaries for being part-time workers as peer educators. In reality, however, they end up working full time but are paid only Rs 1,500 per month.

Even after they take on other jobs, these women are still looked upon as sex workers, and hence people feel they have a right to sexually harass them. Sex workers are sometimes involved in businesses, but few of their jobs are seasonal. Sometimes they have to use other occupations as a ruse to engage in sex work.

Sex workers have expressed the need to be included in social protection schemes and to participate in broader campaigns and forums demanding rights for the unorganized work force. However, income generation schemes at the district level are often conditional on sex workers giving up sex work, a clause that many sex workers reject.

Another factor that impedes participation in income generation schemes is that sex workers are required to be part of self-help groups within their village or where they live. Many sex workers participating in such self-help groups have reported being discriminated and marginalized by other SHG members. Hence the demand for identity-based self help groups needs to be re-considered by the government particularly keeping marginal communities in mind. The Pension Parishad, a national movement to demand Universal Old Age Pension has included the concerns of old sex workers including relaxing the eligibility age to 45 years for highly vulnerable groups such as tribal groups, transgender people and women in sex work.

THE WAY FORWARD

Keeping in mind the above discussion, the following lays out a roadmap for what needs to be done to improve the conditions in which sex workers live and work:

Improved education facilities for children of sex workers

* Special school support program for children of sex workers to be instituted.
* Sex workers' children as well as transchildren (mainly adolescents) should be given the same opportunities to discrimination-free education as other children. All discrimination against them should be dealt with seriousness.
* There should be no insistence on the name of the father in any paperwork at the school. This should be made abundantly clear through a government order to all schools.
* Inability to produce transfer certificates should not be grounds for disallowing a child to join school.
* Teachers and other personnel in hostels, schools and other educational institutions should be sensitized to the issues faced by sex workers' children.
* Sex education that is age-appropriate, scientific and takes on board the concerns of transgendered people and homosexuals to be introduced in all schools.
* Crèche facilities and night shelters for children of sex workers.
* The Right to Education Act should be interpreted to ensure that the children of sex workers and transgender adolescents are also included.

Better preventive and curative health care

* Moving away from the target-driven approach of the HIV program that often promotes or encourages human rights violations.
* Greater emphasis on care and support of sex workers in the HIV program.
* Greater access to gels which are absolutely necessary for anal sex.
* Better access to stigma-free sexual and reproductive health services; access to safe abortion facilities without

discrimination; and right to safe delivery for all, including sex workers who are living with HIV.
- A special scheme to meet the nutritional needs of HIV+ transgenders and sex workers.
- Fighting the rampant discrimination in the public health systems where the personnel from the ward attendants to doctors and the systems within the hospital are insensitive to the transgender and sex worker communities.
- 'Education' to usher in changes in individual behavior, health worker and community perceptions, as well as the training of the health workers to serve without discrimination.
- Rolling out specific programs for sex workers' health and human rights.
- Supporting sex workers' involvement and leadership in all programs, including those addressing SRH and HIV prevention.
- Health issues other than HIV to also receive focus.

Sustainable and exploitation-free livelihood options
- Dubious 'morality' that keeps sex workers ostracized and allows discriminatory laws and policies that prevent sex work from being considered a legitimate livelihood option should cease to exist. These laws need to be unpacked and rewritten.
- Sex workers should enjoy the same protections as workers in other sectors.
- Recognize the rights of all sex workers—female, male and transgender.
- Reforming laws and stopping police repression.
- Stopping raids and involuntary 'rescues'.
- Minimum standards with regard to working conditions in the sex industry, and safeguards against discrimination and violence must be clearly laid down.
- Participation of sex workers' unions in broader federations of labor unions must be improved.

- Sex worker organizations themselves should be centrally involved in all policies that affect them
- Alternative occupations along with or instead of sex work should be made available to those who want them. The policy should do away with forced 'rehabilitation' and all occupational options offered should be done in consultation with those in sex work.
- The National Skills Mission and other concerned authorities should be directed to open up existing schemes to transgenders and sex workers.

Political participation
- Making available election identity cards in the gender of their choice to all transgenders.
- Making provision that allow transgenders to contest elections in the gender of their choice.
- Ensuring that lack of proof of address is not reason to lose access to citizenship rights.
- Creating a mechanism that allows easy registration of collectives of sex workers and of transgenders.

Entitlements
- Removing barriers to access existing schemes including issues around gender identity.
- Social welfare department to provide a variety of social welfare schemes for socially and economically disadvantaged transgenders and sex workers.

Sex Workers Observe May Day

This is the special day for us as we are observing this May Day for the first time not only as sex workers but also as members of 'Karnataka Sex Workers Union', the first sex workers union in Karnataka, perhaps in India. We are diverse and work in diverse environments. We are women, men and hijras. We are from cities, towns and villages. We speak Kannada, Tamil, Telugu, and Urdu. We are Hindus, Muslims, and Christians. We are from different castes, cultures, traditions and socio-political backgrounds. We get into sex work for different reasons. But we have all come together as a Workers' Union to fight for our rights, to get our work recognized as legitimate work with the full range of labor rights.

REFERENCES

Aneka, Karnataka Sex Workers Union, SWaCH, Kagad Kach Patra Kashtakari Panchayat (KKPKP) and Krantijyoti Savitribai Phule Women's Studies Centre (2013), *Redefining Work: Sex Workers and Wastepickers in Conversation*, Bangalore.

Agustín, L. M. (2007), *Sex at the Margins: Migration, Labour Markets and the Rescue Industry*, Zed Books, New York.

Boris, E. and Parreñas, R. S. (eds) (2010), *Intimate Labors: Cultures, Technologies, and the Politics of Care*, Stanford: Stanford University Press.

Fraser, N. (1997), *Justice Interruptus: Critical Reflections on 'Post Socialist' Condition*, London and New York: Routledge.

George, A., Vindhya, U., and Ray, S. (2010), 'Sex trafficking and sex work: Definitions, debates and dynamics—A review of literature', *Economic and Political Weekly*, 45(17), pp. 24–30.

Gothoskar, S. and Kaiwar, A., 'Who Says We Do Not Work', *Economic and Political Weekly*.

Kotiswaran, P. (2011), *Dangerous Sex, Invisible Labor: Sex work and the law in India*, Princeton University Press.

Levine, P. (2004), '"A multitude of unchaste women": Prostitution in the British Empire', *Journal of Women's History*, 15(4), pp. 159–163.

Nair, J. (1994), 'The devadasi, dharma and the state', *Economic and Political Weekly*, 29(50), pp. 3157–3167.

Sahni, R., and Shankar, V.K. (2011), 'The first pan-India survey of sex workers: A summary of preliminary findings', Center for Advocacy on Stigma and Marginalisation.

Sahni, R., and Shankar, V. K. (2013), 'Sex work and its linkages with informal labour markets in India: Findings from the first pan-India survey of female sex workers'.

Shah, S. (2003), 'Sex work in the global economy', *New Labor Forum*, 12, pp. 74–81.

Tambe, A. (2005), 'The elusive ingénue: A transnational feminist analysis of European prostitution in colonial Bombay', *Gender & Society*, 19(2), pp. 160–179.

Vijaisri, P. (2005), 'Contending identities: Sacred prostitution and reform in colonial South India', *South Asia: Journal of South Asian Studies*, 28(3), pp. 387–411.

Weitzer, R. (2007), 'The social construction of sex trafficking: Ideology and institutionalization of a moral crusade', *Politics & Society*, 35(3), pp. 447–475.

WHO (2005), 'Why focus on violence against sex workers and HIV?', in *Violence against sex workers and HIV prevention Information Bulletin Series, Number 3*, World Health Organisation 2005 http://www.who.int/gender/documents/sexworkers.pdf

Food and Nutrition Security in India

The challenges ahead

BIRAJ PATNAIK*

INTRODUCTION

Even though India has emerged as one of the fastest growing economies in the world, it has some of the world's worst social indices. A third of India's children are malnourished, and the proportion of stunted children in India is nearly double that of sub-Saharan Africa. The proportion of low-birth-weight infants, which is also an indicator of the mother's nutritional and health status, is almost twice that of the average for the African continent. India is consistently one of the lowest spenders (as a proportion of the Gross Domestic Product) on education, health care, and other social welfare programs, not just in comparison with countries that are members of the Organisation for Economic Co-operation and Development (OECD) but also in comparison with countries in the Indian subcontinent, like Sri Lanka, Bangladesh and Bhutan. This is reflected in India slipping below Bangladesh in most social indices over the last

---

* Biraj Patnaik is the Principal Adviser to the Commissioners of the Supreme Court in the Right to Food Case (CWP 196/ 2001). The views expressed in this essay are personal.

two decades, ironically the decades of very high (neo-liberal) growth. India seems to have prospered, but Indians clearly have not.

In 2001, the Government of India had a surplus food grain stock of 60 million tonnes, yet a large number of hunger-related deaths were being reported periodically from across the country. The state of Rajasthan had experienced its third successive year of drought, and one of the leading human rights organizations in the country, People's Union for Civil Liberties (PUCL), approached the Supreme Court of India to make the right to food a justiciable right derived from Article 21 of the Indian Constitution, which guarantees the right to life and personal liberty. While the petitioners had asked for relief for the state of Rajasthan, the Supreme Court extended the case across the country, and made all the states/union territories and relevant central government agencies respondents in the case. The National Food Security Act (NFSA) was legislated in 2013, as a result of a long struggle, in the courts and outside, to address this conundrum of hunger amidst plenty (Patnaik and Sinha, 2015).

Status of Malnutrition in India

A comparison between data from the National Family Health Survey 2005–06 (NFHS-3) and from the Rapid Survey on Children (RSOC) 2013-14 shows that there has been notable improvement in the nutritional status of children in the last decade. However, the fact that it has taken seven years for India to generate data on child malnutrition is indicative of the lack of political will to deal with the situation. The status of nutritional surveillance remains abysmally poor despite India possessing a robust statistical infrastructure on all other fronts.

A state-wise analysis of the data reveals that despite the progress, some of the best performing states in India still have

Child Undernutrition in India (%)

	Children below 3 years		Children below 5 years	
	1998–99	2005–06	2005–06	2014–14
Weight-for-age				
Below–2 SD	43	40	43	29
Below–3 SD	18	16	16	9
Height-for-age				
Below–2 SD	51	45	48	39
Below–3 SD	28	22	24	17

Sources: RSOC for 2013-4; NFHS-3 report.

a higher malnutrition rate than even Sudan. Major states like Rajasthan and Gujarat continue to lag behind despite significant progress on the economic front.

Integrated Child Development Services (ICDS)

The only institutional mechanism that India has to deal with the problem of children's malnutrition, for the 160 million children under the age of six and pregnant and nursing mothers, is the Integrated Child Development Services (ICDS). The ICDS provides a basket of six basic services including supplementary feeding for all children under the age of six and all pregnant and nursing mothers in the country, immunization, pre-school education, referral services, and nutrition and health counseling. Even though the program is now close to forty years old, progress has remained uneven, and the charts below show that performance of the states on many parameters remains, at best, sketchy.

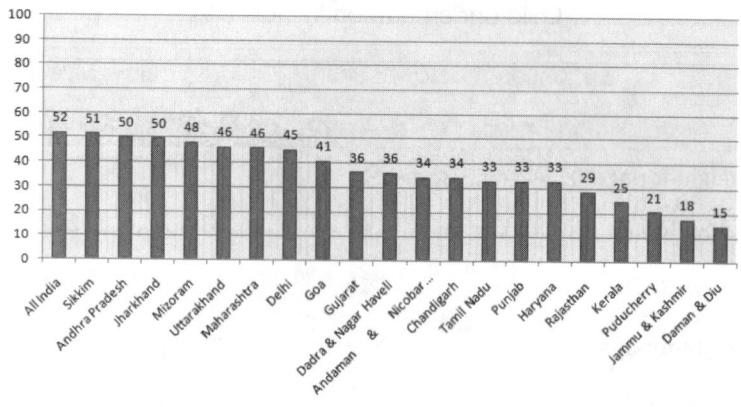

Figure 9.1: States with low coverage of children under SNP

Despite universalization, the supplementary feeding had a coverage of little over 50%.[1] Despite repeated attempts by the Supreme Court and civil society, corruption remains high, especially in the provisioning of complementary foods to children and pregnant and nursing mothers.[2]

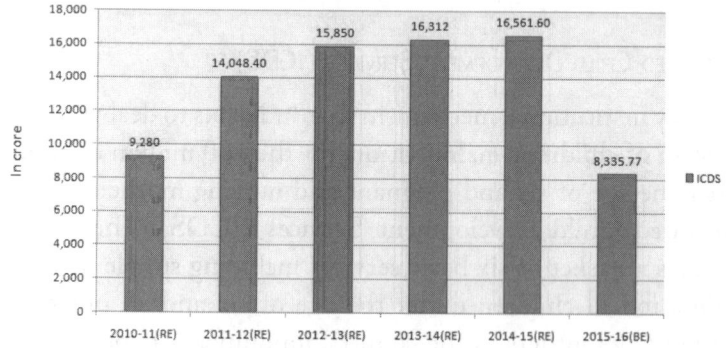

Figure 9.2: ICDS budget

---

[1] ICDS Data Tables, Ministry of Women and Child Development, Government of India

[2] Supreme Court Commissioners' Office: Second report on supply of Take-Home Rations

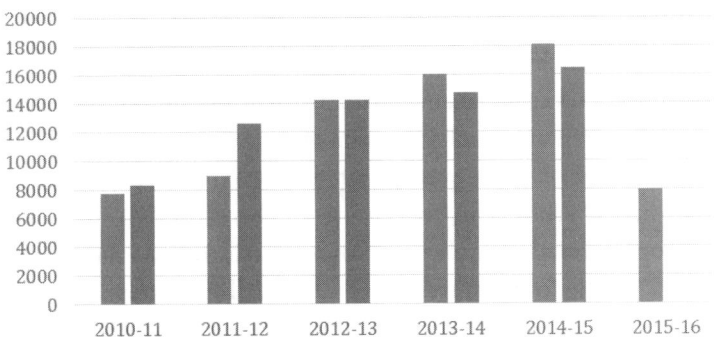

Figure 9.3: ICDS budgetary and revised estimates

More worryingly, the budgetary allocation for the ICDS scheme as well as the overall budget of the Ministry of Women and Child Development (MWCD) has been drastically reduced in the current fiscal year by the NDA government, which would lead to further drops in coverage and effectiveness of the scheme. This is in direct opposition to the need for even higher allocation to protect the ICDS scheme as a legal entitlement promised under the NFSA. After the protests made by the MWCD, the budget has been increased but there is still a huge drop from the previous years' allocation, without even factoring in inflation.

Besides low budgetary allocations, the principal reason for high rates of child malnutrition in India is the failure to address key social determinants like access to potable water, sanitation, and quality primary health care. In addition, the ICDS, as a program, does not focus enough on the needs of children in the first thousand days, which is a critical window of opportunity. Low levels of women's literacy as well as caste and gender discrimination also remain persistent factors contributing to child malnutrition in India.

Mid Day Meal Scheme (MDMS)

Even though the MDMS is one of the better run social sector programs in the country, it still faces severe challenges, not least, the budgetary cuts introduced by the NDA government in 2014-15, which threaten the continuance of the program; and the numerous cases of social exclusion, especially those faced by Dalit children and cooks in India's schools.

In terms of the coverage of the program, there are more than 8,000 schools in the country where the MDMS is still not operational. Quality of the meals served varies across states, with some states and Union Territories like Tamil Nadu, Kerala, Puducherry, Daman and Diu, and Chandigarh

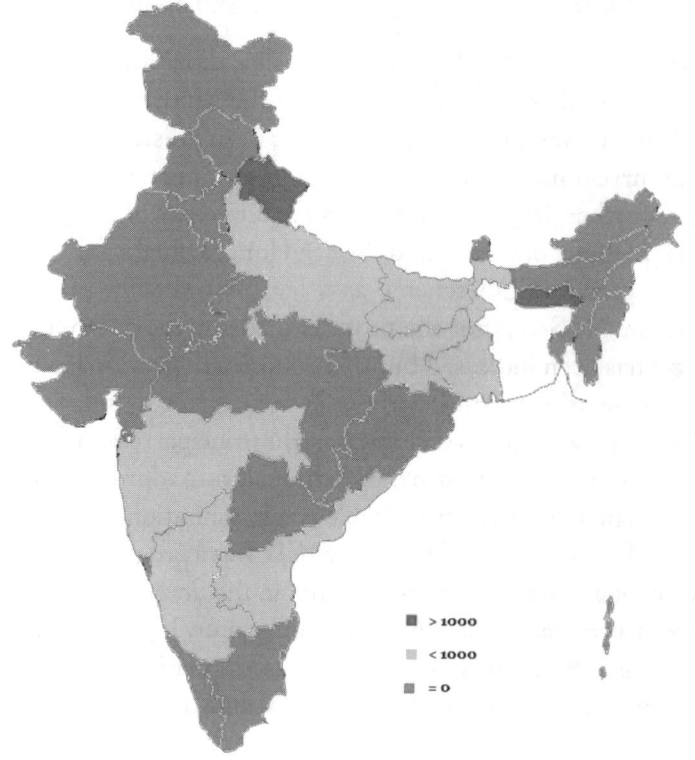

Map 9.1: Schools eligible but not covered under Mid-day Meal

Disclaimer: This figure is not to scale. It does not represent any authentic national or international boundaries and is used for illustrative purpose only.

making significant investments in the program from their own state resources to serve high quality meals. Eggs, which are the primary source of animal protein for many poor children who avail of the MDMS, have been introduced in a number of states including West Bengal and Tamil Nadu.

Of all the food related schemes, the MDMS remains one of the best-monitored programs. Nutritional content of children's meals remains a concern and the absence of data on the nutritional outcomes of the program remains unaddressed. There is evidence, however, of increased enrolment and attendance, especially of girl children, which is heartening.

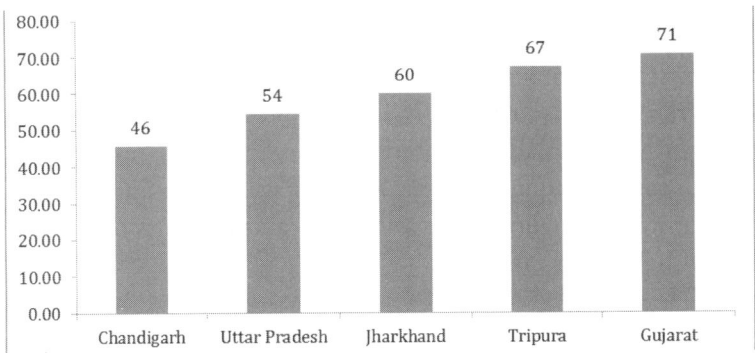

Figure 9.4: Poor performing States on MDM coverage: percentage coverage – enrolment vs. availing

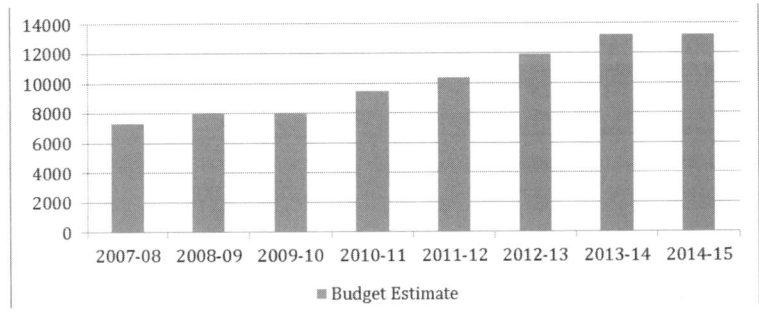

Figure 9.5: Year wise outlay under Mid Day Meal Scheme (Rs in Crores)

As stated earlier, MDMS has seen only a decrease in budgetary allocation from the previous years, which is inadequate to cover even inflation in food prices, let alone facilitate the expansion of the scheme to cover every school going child, as provided for under NFSA.

IMPLEMENTATION OF THE NATIONAL FOOD SECURITY ACT, 2013

Following the life-cycle approach, NFSA will cover more than 820 million people across the country. A short description of the entitlements is given below:

NFSA provides for a free meal (either freshly cooked or ready-to-eat) a day for all children in the age group of six months to six years, and pregnant and nursing women through Anganwadi Centers (AWCSs) run by ICDS. Malnourished children are to be provided an additional meal. The Act also mentions that AWCs must be equipped with drinking water, cooking facilities and sanitation facilities. The following table presents the norms set by the Act for the meals.

Category	Type of Meal	Calories (Kcal)	Protein (g)
Children (six months–three years)	Take Home Ration	500	12–15
Children (three years–six years)	Morning Snack and Hot Cooked Meal	500	12–15
Children (six months–six years) who are malnourished	Take Home Ration	800	20–25
Every Pregnant and Lactating Mother during pregnancy and for six months after childbirth	Take Home Ration	600	18–20

Under MDMS, all the schools run by local bodies as well as those run or aided by the government, are required to provide one free meal every day, with specified nutritional standards, for all children of six to 14 years of age, or up to Class VIII. The guidelines for cooking/procuring these meals are issued by the central government. The meals are to be prepared in the schools in rural areas.

The Act also guarantees a maternity benefit of at least Rs. 6,000 to all pregnant women except those working in government or public-sector undertakings. The central government is required to implement a scheme for the same.

Under the Act, 67% of India's population (75% of the rural population and 50% of the urban population) is entitled to food grains at highly subsidized rates of Rs. 3, Rs. 2 and Re. 1 per kg of wheat, rice and millets, respectively, through the Targeted Public Distribution System (TPDS). The entitlement holders of TPDS have been divided into two categories. The 'priority' category entitles each person in the household to 5 kg of food grains per month, totaling 25 kg per month for a household of five persons. Further, a second category of more vulnerable persons is defined by state governments, as per guidelines from the central government, and covered under the Antyodaya Anna Yojana. Under this category, the rates offered to the beneficiaries are the same, but each household is entitled to 35 kg of food grains, irrespective of its size.[3]

Maternity Entitlements under NFSA

Maternity benefits are an obligation of the government, as it is a signatory to several international instruments, such as the International Labour Organization (ILO) Maternity Protection

---

[3] Supreme Court Commissioners' Office: Second report on supply of Take-Home Rations

Convention; International Covenant on Economic, Social and Cultural Rights (ICESCR); the Convention on the Elimination of all Forms of Discrimination Against Women (CEDAW); as well as Article 39 and Article 42 of the Constitution of India. The government has attempted to meet these obligations through several schemes, such as the National Maternity Benefit Scheme (NMBS); the Janani Suraksha Yojana (JSY); some state government schemes for the unorganized sector; and provisions under the Maternity Benefit Act for the organized sector.

The first central government scheme to provide cash maternity benefit to women as wage compensation was introduced in 2010 as the Indira Gandhi Matritva Sahyog Yojana (IGMSY), and provided for a conditional cash transfer of Rs. 4,000. The scheme is being implemented on a pilot basis in 53 districts in the country and provides cash entitlement to women above the age of 18 years for up to two live births.

The National Food Security Act, in adopting a life-cycle approach and in recognizing food and nutritional needs, provided for a cash entitlement of Rs. 6,000 to all pregnant and lactating women who are not working in the formal sector. The IGMSY was amended to cater to the NFSA, and the cash entitlement was increased from Rs. 4,000 to Rs. 6,000.[4] Despite being a legal entitlement under the NFSA, the benefit is limited to only the 53 districts where IGMSY is being implemented. The benefit was to become universal and provided in all districts of the country from the date of NFSA coming into force, i.e., 5 July 2013, but no budgetary allocations have been made for its expansion to other districts. The Right to Food Campaign (RTFC) and the National Alliance for Maternal Health and Human Rights (NAMHHR) have been campaigning for the expansion of the scheme to all districts of the country, while PUCL has also filed

---

[4] Letter dated 27.09.2013 from Ministry of Women and Child Development, Government of India

a petition in the Supreme Court demanding that all pregnant and lactating women should retrospectively and henceforth receive the cash entitlements (from 5 July 2013).[5]

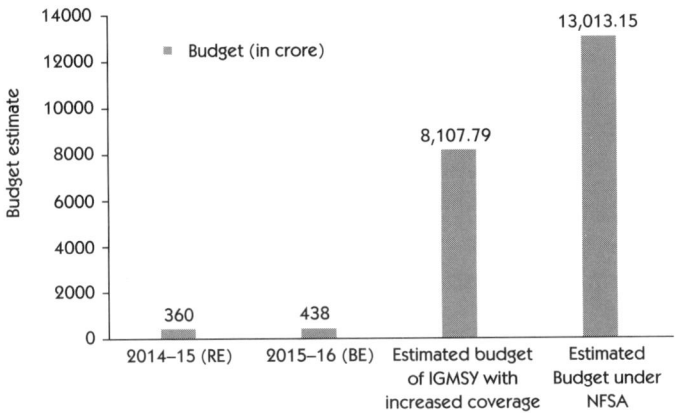

Figure 9.6: IGMSY Budget

However, the maternity entitlement program remains the most poorly funded scheme under NFSA, with the central government's budget allocation for the scheme being less than 3.5% of the requirement.

In addition, NFSA does not prescribe any eligibility criteria to receive the entitlement—the benefit should be available to all women except those who are employed in the formal sector. However, the current scheme under IGMSY provides the entitlement to women only above the age of 19 years and for up to two live childbirths, and thereby excludes 38% of the women who would otherwise be eligible. The exclusion is even higher among Scheduled Caste (SC) and Scheduled Tribe (ST) women (41% and 47%, respectively), who are even more vulnerable and in greater need of the entitlement. The government has also proposed the additional conditionality of being a 'priority' or

---

[5] PUCL vs. Union of India and others, Supreme Court Writ Petition (Civil) no. 277 of 2015

'antyodaya' household to be eligible to receive the benefit. Such conditionalities breach the mandate of NFSA, which provides for universal entitlement to maternity benefits.

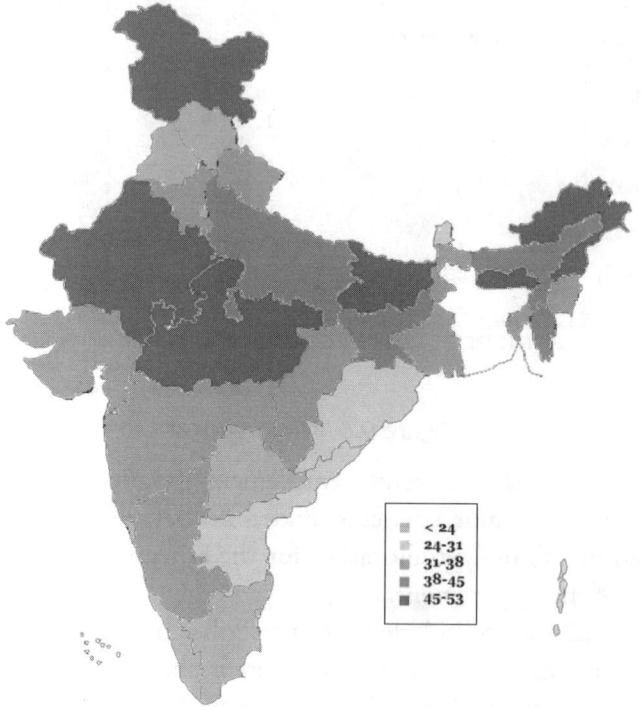

Map 9.2: Exclusion from IGMSY (Maternity Entitlements Schemes in India) due to Eligibility Criteria

Disclaimer: This figure is not to scale. It does not represent any authentic national or international boundaries and is used for illustrative purpose only.

On the positive side, the Law Commission of India's report (LCI, 2015) has recommended that the provision of maternity benefits be made obligatory on the State and not left to the will of the employers. The report also recommends that the entitlement should cover all women, including those employed in the unorganized sector.

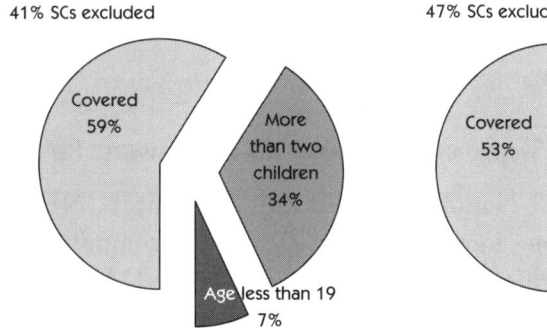
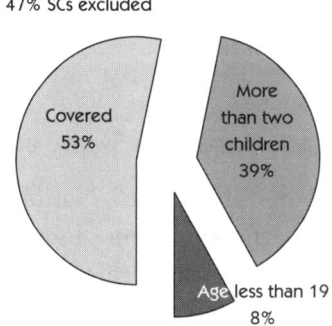

Figure 9.7a: Exclusion among SCs due to IGMSY eligibility criteria

Figure 9.7b: Exclusion among STs due to IGMSY eligibility criteria

Socio-Economic Caste Census, 2011 and the Challenge of Identifying the Poor for Social Security Programs

The standard poverty line method to identify the beneficiaries of the TPDS, before the ratification of NFSA, had been a subject of long-standing and complex debate. In order to overcome the challenges posed to the poverty line method and also improve identification of the poor/beneficiaries, the government initiated the Socio-Economic Caste Census (SECC), 2011. It was expected that most states would use the data from SECC for the identification of entitlement holders.

SECC was originally intended to be completed by 2011. NFSA provides that the identification of beneficiaries for the purposes of the Act must be completed within 365 days of the commencement of the Act.

While SECC data is more robust than that of earlier surveys, it should only be used for excluding the rich and not for deciding on the inclusion of the poor. All those who are not excluded by the criteria set by the SECC survey should get the benefits of NFSA. With the expanded coverage under NFSA, this can easily be done in most poor states. In fact, states such as Bihar and Odisha are doing precisely this. Madhya Pradesh, on the other hand, has used a different database created by the state government (called the SAMAGRA portal) to identify cardholders.

Public Distribution System and the Shanta Kumar Committee Report

Soon after the National Democratic Alliance (NDA) Government came into power, it created a committee—headed by the former Food Minister in the last NDA regime, Shanta Kumar—to make recommendations to restructure the operations of the Food Corporation of India (FCI). FCI is responsible for the procurement, storage and distribution of food grains in India. Even though it was neither the mandate of the committee nor mentioned in its terms of reference, the committee made sweeping recommendations to whittle down NFSA. These recommendations included reducing the coverage of the entitlement holders from 67% to 40%, and raising the issue price of the food grains to peg it to the Minimum Support Price paid to the farmers. It also recommended a gradual shift to cash transfers to farmers and consumers, instead of providing them with food grains. While the government has not explicitly stated whether these recommendations will be accepted, this reflects the thinking of the current establishment, which could jeopardize not just the infrastructure for the delivery of the right to food, but also the architecture of welfare in India. The central government has been lax in pulling up the states to implement NFSA, and has repeatedly (and illegally) extended the deadline for implementation. As of November 2015, only 18 states in the country have started implementing NFSA (LCI, 2015).

Although India's food subsidy figures have shown a consistent rise, it must be noted that they remains below 1% of the GDP. Many states have shown drastic improvement in the performance of the Public Distribution System (PDS) over the last few years. These states include Chhattisgarh, Bihar, Odisha, Tamil Nadu, Himachal Pradesh, Kerala and Andhra Pradesh.

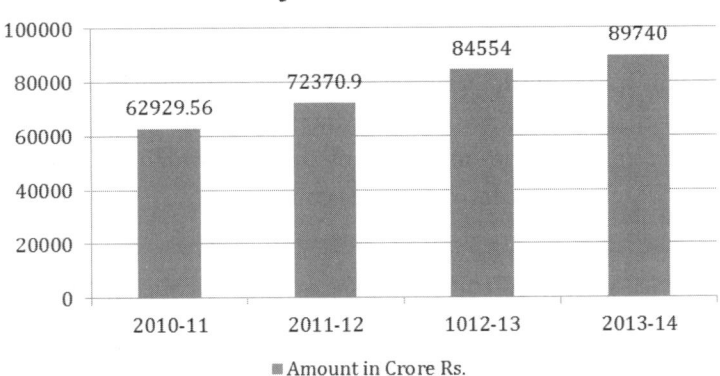

Figure 9.8: Subsidy on food grains

Source: Annual Report 2013–14 of DFPD

Despite the strategic buffer limit being set at around 25 million metric tonnes, as the stock position figures below reflect, India holds food grains far in excess of the required buffer limit. This is primarily due to the non-implementation of NFSA across the country. One of the moves of the NDA government

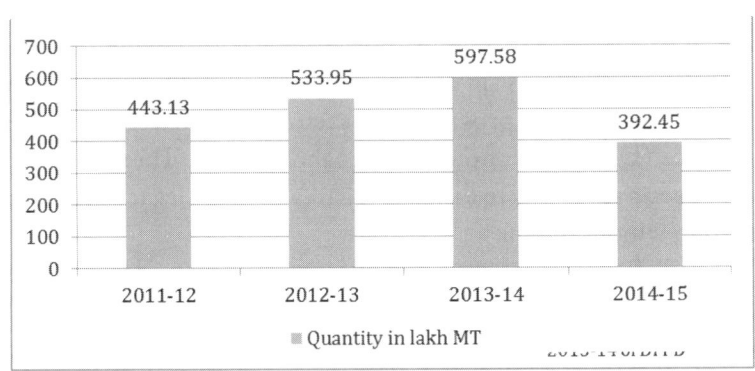

Figure 9.9: Stock position of foodgrains in central pool

Source: Annual Report 2013–14 of DFPD

in 2014 was to limit the procurement of food grains under the Minimum Support Price mechanism by state governments. This has aggravated the agrarian crisis in India, especially in states like Chhattisgarh, Madhya Pradesh and Rajasthan, where farmers are dealing with the onslaught of drought and/or unseasonal rains, which impact farm incomes considerably.

PDS Control Order (2015) and the Threat to the NFSA[6]

First, the Antyodaya Anna Yojana (AAY) is being sought to be phased out, with states being instructed not to add any new household to this category if any household drops out of the program due to an improvement in social or economic status, death, etc. This means that the number of households covered under AAY can only decrease, and that over time, the program will be phased out. AAY provides 35 kg of food grains per month (irrespective of the number of members in the household) to 20 million of the most vulnerable families in the country, and is currently accessed by the most vulnerable tribal communities, persons with disability, and the aged. Launched on then Prime Minister of India Mr. Atal Bihari Vajpayee's birthday 15 years ago, when the NDA was in power, it was a scheme that he took personal interest in and nurtured through his tenure. The effectiveness of the program led even the United Progressive Alliance (UPA) government to expand it twice. There couldn't have been a surer way to disrespect Mr. Vajpayee's legacy program than to wind it down.

Second, in complete contravention of the orders of the Supreme Court and NFSA (Section 9), the PDS (Control) Order freezes the number of people who can access the entitlements to the decadal Census figures, rather than expand

---

[6] This section is from, Patnaik, B, 'Cutting the Food Act to the Bone', *The Hindu*, June 24th, 2015

it each year based on the population estimates of the Registrar General and Census Commissioner of India. What this means is that state governments cannot add to the number of beneficiaries to accommodate the increase in population in the 10-year period between the publication of the final Census results.

Most damningly, for the first time, the PDS (Control) Order explicitly places an additional burden of citizenship, besides being a resident of the State, for someone to access benefits under NFSA. Ostensibly, this is to check foreigners, (especially the large number of Canadians who are perhaps queuing up at our ration shops!) to get the benefits of PDS. In practical terms, what this means is that some of the most vulnerable migrant communities of India would find themselves excluded from PDS. And if you thought this was an entirely theoretical proposition, try getting a ration card in Delhi if you are a Bengali migrant who also happens to have a Muslim name. Well, try getting yourself a ration card anyway. The last PDS (Control) Order issued in 2001 did not think it necessary to make this distinction, nor did NFSA, where the entitlements are defined for 'persons' rather than citizens. Since the jurisprudence on the right to food flows from Article 21 of the Constitution, on the right to life and personal liberty, the right to food should be available to all persons without their having to establish their citizenship first.

The impact of these measures is already being felt across the country, with the visibly weakening political will of the central government impacting program implementation in the field. Chhattisgarh's PDS, arguably one of the best in the country—even the Supreme Court has repeatedly highlighted it as an example that other states should emulate—is tainted by a procurement scam. Close to 700,000 ration cards have been cancelled. While a large number of them were subsequently reinstated, the most marginalized sections of the population have not managed to find their way back into the system.

The Ongoing Debate of Food Entitlements versus Cash Entitlements[7]

Through the Economic Survey 2014–15 and the Budget 2015, the present central government has conveyed that the main policy instrument through which poverty reduction will be achieved in the country is Direct Benefit Transfers (DBT). One of the main DBT schemes that is being discussed is a proposal to replace the distribution of food grains through PDS with cash transfers. In this policy brief, we assess the pros and cons of this proposal.

Under the PDS, households are provided highly subsidized food grains through a network of fair price shops (FPSs). Currently, the coverage, quantity and prices under which PDS grains are distributed are decided on the basis of NFSA. The state governments are responsible for the implementation of the Act, while the food grains are allocated by the Government of India. The states have formulated their own eligibility criteria to identify households which should come under the 'priority' category, which is to be capped at 75% of rural areas and 50% of urban areas for the country, with variations across states.

With regard to introducing DBTs in PDS, the central government has asked state governments to consider starting pilots. One of the pre-conditions for introducing DBTs is to complete digitization of beneficiary data and seed it with Aadhaar (Unique Identifcation Number, or UID). As of now, pilots have been initiated in three union territories (UTs)—Chandigarh, Puducherry and Dadra and Nagar Haveli. There is also a small pilot in the city of Raipur in Chhattisgarh. While these are recent developments and the experiences of these pilots are yet to be studied, there are a number of issues related to replacing PDS with cash transfers, which need to be kept in mind.

---

[7] This section is from, Sinha, D. and Patnaik, B. (2015). *Oxfam Policy Brief 2015: Cash for Food: The Need for Caution*

Concerns have been raised that replacing the provision of food grains with cash will not ensure that the money will address food insecurity. The poor face a number of vulnerabilities and the cash could be spent on other urgent needs. Second, with rising food prices there is a danger that the value of the cash transfer will decline over time unless a very robust system of inflation-indexing is put in place. Third, in spite of the Pradhan Mantri Jan-Dhan Yojana, there are still large bottlenecks in access to banks for the poor, whereas the network of FPSs is far more widespread and more easily accessible. Fourth, the withdrawing of the provision of grains through PDS comes with the danger of reduction in procurement at MSP. At a time when agriculture is in crisis and there are very few arenas of support available to farmers, such a move could be disastrous. Fifth, targeting errors that were part of the earlier PDS can now be addressed—exclusion errors through expanded coverage under the NFSA, and inclusion errors through using data from the verified SECC lists for identification. There is nothing inherent in cash transfers that makes targeting foolproof. Finally, leakages in PDS are showing a declining trend, based on which it can be safely predicted that, with NFSA implementation in all states, the leakages in PDS will only come down further. Therefore, this is not the time to dismantle PDS, rather to strengthen state governments' efforts to improve it.

No matter how much faith the union government may have on them, the pilots initiated to introduce DBTs/cash transfers in PDS have largely failed across states. A study of the pilot started in six shops across three cities in Chhattisgarh found that a fifth of the beneficiary households never received any money, and among those who did, 70% did so after much delay. Further, 43% faced financial distress in trying to buy PDS rice during the pilot and one-third had difficulties related to getting Aadhaar numbers and/or bank accounts. In Puducherry, the first attempt at introducing cash transfers had to be withdrawn within two months in response to large scale protests by people. The UT has now made another attempt, where it retains a part of the grain transfer and cash is being given only in lieu of a portion of the grains. An earlier attempt at introducing DBTs in the distribution of kerosene through a pilot scheme in Kotkasim, Rajasthan was also largely a failure.

One of the main arguments proposed in favor of cash transfers in PDS is the high level of leakages in PDS. However, what is ignored is the decline in leakages that is being seen in PDS since 2004–05. While the leakages in PDS were to the tune of 54% in 2004–05, they have come down to between 35% and 42% (depending on which estimates are considered) in 2011–12. Further, some states such as Tamil Nadu, Andhra Pradesh and Chhattisgarh show much lower levels of leakage. States that have introduced more recent reforms in the PDS, such as Odisha, Madhya Pradesh and Bihar, are also showing great improvement with respect to PDS leakages.

All these states where leakages are on a decline have some common features, such as expansion in coverage, uniform and low prices, reforms such as computerization, door-step delivery, enhanced transparency, and provisions for grievance redressal. With NFSA, these reforms can be replicated in other states as well and a further decline in PDS can be expected by the time the next round of data is available.

Conclusions

While considerable progress has been made on the food and nutrition security front in India, the challenges remain daunting. On the positive side, NFSA has made specific provisions for maternity entitlements and also legislated that all ration cards should be issued in the name of women. Yet, this would remain tokenistic in the absence of more concrete measures to address the structural issues related to gender discrimination in India.

Also on the positive side, there is hope that the Swachh Bharat Abhiyan, with all its flaws, will eventually have a drastic impact on the poor sanitation record in the country, and especially improve women's access to private toilets.

Yet, as the preceding sections show, the severe budget cuts, lack of political will and the series of retrograde steps taken by the government may end up making NFSA just another legislation on paper.

References

Patnaik, B. and Sinha, Dipa (2015). *Oxfam Policy Brief 2015: National Food Security Act.*

Law Commission of India, Report No.259, August 2015, Early Childhood Development and Legal Entitlements.

Patnaik, B, 'Cutting the Food Act to the Bone', *The Hindu*, 24 June 2015.

Sinha, D., and Patnaik, B. (2015). *Oxfam Policy Brief 2015: Cash for Food: The Need for Caution.*

Supreme Court Commissioners' Office: Second report on supply of Take Home Rations. http://sccommissioners.org/Reports/Reports/Second%20Report%20on%20Status%20of%20Supply%20of%20THR%20by%20Principal%20Adviser.pdf

Maternity Entitlements in India

An overview

Yamini Atmavilas[*]

INTRODUCTION

Maternity entitlements refer to cash and non-cash benefits and care to women during pregnancy and the antenatal period, childbirth, and the postnatal period until women are expected to require rest and care from a medical perspective. Conceptually and programmatically, maternity brings together the economic and the social, the productive and the reproductive, the medical and the social. Maternity protection has two aims: to preserve the health of the mother and the newborn; and to provide a measure of job security (protection from dismissal and discrimination, the right to resume work after birth, and maintenance of wages and benefits during maternity). The need for maternity entitlements cannot be overemphasized. Policy frameworks need to encompass and go beyond the labor and work/non-work and

---

[*] The research undertaken for this essay was conducted during the author's tenure as Chair, Gender Studies, Administrative Staff College of India. The essay expresses neither the views of the Administrative Staff College of India, nor of the Bill and Melinda Gates Foundation. All views and opinions, and errors, if any, are the author's own.

health frameworks where maternity entitlements have typically been framed.

Context: Need for Broad-based Maternity Entitlements and Protection in India

There are at least three key framing contextual realities to the question of maternity and maternity entitlements in India:

- Preponderance of informality in women's labor
- High levels of maternal morbidity and mortality
- Relationship between poverty and expenditure on health, including maternity

Firstly, we know that poor women lack access to decent work that enables them to work under safe or secure conditions, and mainly balance care work with work in the informal sector, which is characterized by lack of any maternity or labor protection and poor standards of work. 96% of women workers in India, estimated at 142 million in the National Sample Survey 64th Round 2004–05 (NCEUS, 2007), are part of the unorganized sector, which is not covered by labor laws, and therefore not eligible for maternity benefits or comprehensive maternity protection.

The most productive years of a woman's life are also the reproductive years. In the absence of effective maternity protection, a woman worker would have to leave her job to have her child. Poor health, additional medical expenses and loss of employment make the woman worker economically and physically vulnerable during the period of pregnancy and childbirth. Loss of income may force some families to borrow from money lenders, plunging them into a debt crisis. The woman worker may not take adequate rest and start working soon after childbirth, with adverse effects on her health. The repeated neglect of a woman's health during pregnancy and childbirth manifests itself in high mortality rates.

Table 1: Share of States' Maternal Mortality Rates to Total Maternal Deaths

Region	MMR	% Total Maternal Deaths
EAG States* and Assam	308	61.6
Southern States	127	11.4
Other States	149	27
India	212	100

* Empowered Action Group states: Bihar, Jharkhand, Chhattissgarh, MP, Odisha, Rajasthan, UP, Uttarakhand

Secondly, high levels of morbidity and mortality characterize maternity in India for poor women. Every third woman is undernourished and every second woman is anaemic. Poverty and poor access to nutrition and health care contribute to this alarming reality. Gender discriminatory customary norms and existing gender roles also burden women's time and energy and disallow rest. Women's limited access to health care and nutrition reduces their chances for healthy childbearing. Early marriage and poor access to contraception result in, and contribute to, lower bargaining power and influence within the marital relationship, and multiple births and the risk of death after several pregnancies is very real. Each year, more than half a million women die from causes related to pregnancy and childbirth (UNICEF, 2008). Further, for every woman who dies from pregnancy-related complications, around 20 more incur injuries, infections and disabilities. The average lifetime risk of a woman in a least developed country dying from pregnancy or childbirth related complications is estimated to be 300 times greater than for a woman living in an industrialized country.

Sample Registration System data from 2007–09 on maternal mortality shows that India's Maternal Mortality Rate (MMR) is 212 per 100,000 live births (compared to 14 in industrialized countries). It also shows that just eight out of 25 states and union territories in the country with poor economic and human development, grouped together as the Empowered Action Group states (Bihar, Jharkhand, Chhattisgarh, MP, Odisha, Rajasthan, UP, Uttarakhand), contribute nearly two-thirds of maternal deaths in the country.

Map 10.1: Regional Variations in MMR 2007–09: Special Bulletin (2011) on Maternal Mortality in India 2007–09 (SRS) Office of Registrar General, India

Disclaimer: This figure is not to scale. It does not represent any authentic national or international boundaries and is used for illustrative purpose only.

Thirdly, there is a well-established relationship between health expenditure and poverty in poor households. Estimates based on National Sample Survey Organization (NSSO) data suggest that anywhere between 39 million people (Selvaraj and Karan, 2009), and 63 million individuals or 11.9 million households (Berman et al., 2010) were pushed below the poverty line (BPL) by health care expenditure in 2004. Approximately 14% of households in rural areas and 12% in urban areas spend more than 10% of their total annual consumption expenditure on health care (MSPI, 2004). When we look at the incidence and intensity of 'catastrophic' maternal health care expenditure and its socio-economic correlates, we find that after adjusting for out-of-pocket maternal health care expenditure, the poverty in urban and rural areas increased by almost equal percentage points (20% in urban areas versus 19% in rural areas). Maternal health care expenditure in urban households was almost twice that of rural households; a little more than one third households suffered catastrophic payments in both urban and rural areas; rural women from scheduled tribes (ST) had more catastrophic head counts than ST women from urban areas; the catastrophic head count was greater among illiterate women living in urban areas compared to those living in rural areas.

Given these multiple realities, the state has sought to address maternity entitlements in different ways, prioritizing distinct deprivations. Some of them are discussed in the next section.

Current Policy Attention: An Overview

What the Indian state provides by way of maternity entitlements includes provisions of cash and in-kind (nutrition, health services) transfers, insurance support, and labor laws extending wages and leave. These can be, for the sake of simplicity, mapped into three categories (albeit, some might consider these overlapping):

Table 2: Policy Framework for Maternity Entitlements

Conceptual and Policy Framework	Programs
Health/Nutrition Framework	• Integrated Childcare Development Services (ICDS) – Supplementary Nutrition for pregnant and lactating (P&L) mothers • Janani Suraksha Yojana (JSY) – Institutional deliveries and conditional cash transfers (CCT) • Indira Gandhi Matritva Sahayog Yojana (IGMSY)
Insurance Framework	• Rashtriya Swasthya Bima Yojana (RSBY) • Central Government Health Scheme (CGHS)
Labor Framework	• Employees' State Insurance (ESI) Act • Maternity Benefits Act • Mahatma Gandhi National Rural Employment Guarantee Act (MGNREGA) New Guidelines

Maternity Benefits in a Labor Framework

In a labor perspective, often the traditional social security frame, the state guarantees maternity benefits under the Maternity Benefits Act, 1961 and the Employees' State Insurance (ESI) Act, 1948. In addition, the MGNREGA provides for less strenuous work and crèches for pregnant and lactating women on the rolls. A summary of provisions in the labor framework is in the table below. Presently the ESI Act applies to employees who are earning up to Rs. 10,000 a month (approx. USD250), and employers are obliged to uniformly cover men and women. The Maternity Benefits Act, 1961 is applicable to all workers in the organized sector who are not covered under the Employees' State Insurance Act. Data from NSSO (61st round) shows that female workers aged 15–49 who are eligible for maternity benefits form a mere 3% of workers (Lingam and Yelamanchili, 2011). Hence, the reach of maternity benefit schemes on the basis of employment status is very small, and excludes the majority of poor women who work outside the organized sector. The Guidelines of the MGNREGA do provide that pregnant and lactating women (at least up to eight months before delivery and 10 months after delivery) should be treated as a special category, with a mandate for the provisioning of special work which is less strenuous and close to their homes. They also provide for a crèche for children of women wage laborers. In addition there is also provision for treatment and compensation in case of accident, disability or death due to work. Implementation across the states, however, has been varying.

Table 3: Maternity-related Labor Provisions

ESI Act	• Applicable to non seasonal factories using power and employing ten or more persons and non power using non seasonal factories employing twenty or more persons (e.g., shops). • Maternity Benefit is payable to an insured woman (or pregnant woman) in the following cases subject to contributory conditions: Confinement is payable for a period of 12 weeks (84 days) and miscarriage or MTP (Medical Termination of Pregnancy) is payable for 6 weeks (42 days) from the date following miscarriage; maternity benefit rate is double the Standard Benefit Rate, or is roughly equal to the average daily wage.
Maternity Benefits Act	• Applicable to women working in establishments engaging 10 or more persons; and not applicable to any factory or other establishments to which the provisions of the Employees' State Insurance Act, 1948 apply. • Prohibits employment of, or work by, women during the six weeks period immediately following the day of her delivery or miscarriage. • Entitles women workers to maternity benefit at specified rates for specified periods.

MGNREGA New Guidelines	• Pregnant and lactating women (at least upto eight months before delivery and 10 months after delivery) delineated as a special category, with a mandate for the provisioning of special work which is less strenuous and close to their homes; provision for crèche for children of women wage laborers. • In addition there is also provision for treatment and compensation in case of accident, disability or death due to work.

Maternity Benefits in a Health Insurance Framework

Within the health insurance framework, the Rashtriya Swasthya Bima Yojana (RSBY) is the only scheme that provides maternity coverage limited to hospital costs. Since 2007, a new wave of government-sponsored health insurance schemes, like Rajiv Aarogyasri Community Health Insurance Scheme, has introduced a new set of arrangements to govern, allocate, and manage the use of public resources for health, including an explicit (and delivered) package of services, greater accountability for delivering services, and a bottom-up design to reach universal coverage by first achieving coverage of the poor. These insurance schemes are demand-side schemes aimed at improving public purchasing of inpatient services for the poor and focused on providing secondary and tertiary care.

RSBY was launched as a national health insurance scheme in April 2008 targeted at BPL families and by September 2012, the RSBY had enrolled over 32 million families from 25 states for inpatient treatment. The coverage requires no premium contribution or copayment to be made by the beneficiary, and is 'cashless'. More than 10,000 hospitals have been empanelled in the scheme and thirteen insurance companies (both public and private sector) implement the scheme. The central coordinating and policy-making agency for the RSBY is the Government of India's Ministry of Labour and Employment (MOLE).

Table 4: Comparison of RSBY and State Insurance schemes for key provisions

Insurance Scheme	Chronic Diseases	Maternity	Preventive and Wellness Care	AYUSH	Out Patient	In Patient
CGHS	✓	✓	✓	✓	✓	✓
ESIS	✓	✓	✓	✓	✓	✓
Yeshaswini	✓	×	×	×	×	✓
Rajiv Aarogyasri Community Health Insurance Scheme (AP)	✓	×	×	×	except free consultations	✓
RSBY	✓	✓	×	×	×	✓
Kalaignar	✓	×	×	×	×	✓
Vajpayee Aarogyasri Scheme (KN)	✓	×	×	×	×	✓

Source: Public Health Foundation of India. 2011. A Critical Assessment of the Existing Health Insurance Models in India. Sponsored under the Scheme of Socio-Economic Research, The Planning Commission of India, New Delhi.

A nominal yearly adherence fee of Rs. 30 (approx. USD 0.5) per family of five is paid by the BPL household itself.

Reliable figures for the number of maternity hospitalizations are hard to come by; however, there is some gender-related data available that gives us a very mixed picture. As the table below shows, the proportion of women beneficiaries has been increasing year after year.

Table 5: Beneficiaries under RSBY

Round	Male	Female
Round 1	60%	40%
Round 2	56%	44%
Round 3	52%	48%

Hospitalization figures show that the number of women using hospital services is increasing, and hospitalization ratio figures—measured in terms of those who avail hospitalization facilities as compared to those who are enrolled—also appear to show an improvement in women's hospitalizations.[1] When we look at a more disaggregated picture from the states, we find some gender disparities. For instance, an evaluation of RSBY from Gujarat shows that while the sex ratio of the enrolled households in the baseline was 947/1000, the insured sex ratio was 868/1000 and uninsured sex ratio was 1159/1000. In other words, fewer women were enrolled in the scheme than eligible. Awareness of maternity coverage was also low. Other states too showed fewer female beneficiaries, like Kerala (55.7% male; 44.3% female) and Haryana (54% male; 46% female). While further work needs to be done, the example of Gujarat clearly shows that household gender disparities play a role in women's ability to avail the insurance benefit because the scheme design

---

[1] Gender-related figures from December 2012: http://pib.nic.in/archieve/others/2012/dec/d2012120605.pdf

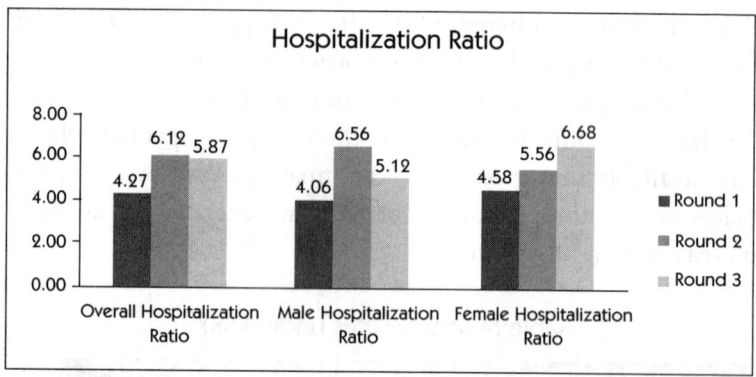

Figure 10.1: Male-Female Hospitalization Ratio by Round under RSBY

Source: Gender-related figures from December 2012: http://pib.nic.in/archieve/others/2012/dec/d2012120605.pdf

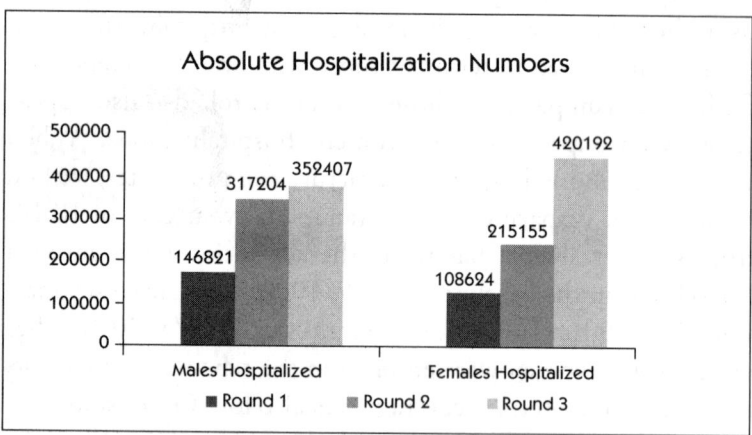

Figure 10.2: Increase in Male-Female Absolute Hospitalizations by Round under RSBY

Source: Gender-related figures from December 2012: http://pib.nic.in/archieve/others/2012/dec/d2012120605.pdf

leaves the mix of enrolled members to be decided by the head of the household. The enrolments are flexible and can change every year, a positive attribute. However, the risk of women and girls being left out is real.

Maternity Benefits in a Health and Nutrition Framework

The Supplementary Nutrition Programme (SNP), under the Integrated Child Development Services (ICDS), is the longest standing component of the Health and Nutrition framework. It is an unconditional in-kind transfer to mothers for 300 days in a year. The ICDS currently covers about 15 million (1.5 crore) mothers through the Anganwadi platform. By providing supplementary feeding, the Anganwadi attempts to bridge the protein energy gap between the recommended dietary allowance and average dietary intake of children and women. Women's self-help groups have also emerged as a vehicle for economic and social empowerment of women; accordingly, synergy between women's self-help groups and the ICDS program would be an emerging aspect in the coming years. There are also many similar state-level initiatives, such as Kulavilakku Scheme in Puducherry, and Indiramma Amrutha Hastham of the Government of Andhra Pradesh.

Under this umbrella, schemes based on conditional cash transfers[2] have also been designed and implemented at the central and state levels. A conditional cash transfer program presumes that low utilization of a particular service is the result of a lack of demand. Demand barriers to accessing health care can include: education of the recipient, lack of knowledge or

---

[2] A conditional cash transfer (CCT) is a scheme whereby usually a monetary benefit is given to a person once certain conditions have been met. These schemes usually target areas such as education, health or nutrition. The aim of a conditional cash transfer is to increase the utilization of services by offering incentives.

information of the service, location of the service, cost of the service both financially and in time, and barriers due to cultural norms. Supply factors that reduce access to services can include: lack of skilled staff; lack of technology, equipment and drugs; expectation of bribes; abuse or discrimination of patients by staff; infrastructural barriers to reaching the service; and perhaps most importantly, the availability of the service.

Janani Suraksha Yojana (JSY) is a conditional cash transfer program to improve maternal survival under the National Rural Health Mission (NRHM). It provides all pregnant women in rural areas who deliver in a health facility, a cash transfer of Rs. 1,400 at or immediately after the delivery to defray the expenses. Institutional deliveries in India have since expanded from 53% of all deliveries in 2005 to 73% in 2009–10 (UNICEF 2005, 2009).

JSY, however, does not directly address the issues regarding a woman's socio-economic compulsions to work right up to the last stage of pregnancy and resuming work soon after childbirth. Hence, a modest maternity benefit to partly compensate for their wage loss was recommended by the Planning Commission in the Eleventh Five-Year Plan and a pilot of the Indira Gandhi Matritva Sahayog Yojana (IGMSY) scheme was launched by the Ministry of Women and Child Development (MWCD) using the platform of ICDS and through the Anganwadi Centre (AWC).

The scheme is designed as a conditional cash transfer and provides a cash benefit to women during pregnancy and lactation in response to individuals fulfilling specific conditions. The scheme attempts to partly compensate for wage loss to Pregnant & Lactating women both prior to and after delivery of the child. It seeks to combine short-term income support objectives with the longer-term objective of behaviour and attitudinal change by linking the benefits to specific nutrition and health-related conditionalities. By routing the installments through bank and postal accounts, the scheme also aims to promote the financial inclusion of women.

The scheme seeks to address the maternity benefit needs of women in the informal sector where they receive none. Typically, maternity benefits are extended to women for compensating for wage loss during pregnancy and to ensure that the woman is not compelled to work and is able to negotiate for rest in the advanced stages of pregnancy and post-childbirth in particular. The amount of incentive was calculated to cover a wage loss compensation of approximately 40 days at Rs. 100 per day. 40 days is the typical length of rest or 'confinement' culturally observed in most regions of the country.

The scheme is being implemented initially on a pilot basis in 53 selected districts using the ICDS platform. Coverage in these districts has been 0.37 million pregnant and lactating women in 2012–13, and about 1.2 million P&L women are expected to be covered every year under the IGMSY. Beneficiaries receive Rs. 4000 in three installments between the second trimester and the child attaining the age of 6 months, based on the fulfillment of a set of specific conditions related to maternal and child health which are summarized below.

Table 6: Conditions for Installments

Cash Transfer	*Conditions*
Rs. 1500 (at the end of second trimester)	i. Registration of pregnancy within four months ii. Antenatal check-up (minimum one)—including IFA and TT iii. Attending counseling session/s (minimum one)
Rs. 1500 (three months after delivery)	i. Childbirth registration ii. Immunization—OPV and BCG at birth, OPV and DPT at six weeks, OPV and DPT at 10 weeks iii. Attending growth monitoring and counseling sessions

Cash Transfer	Conditions
Rs. 1000 (six months after delivery)	i. Exclusive breastfeeding for six months and introduction of complementary feeding (self-certification by mother) ii. Immunization—OPV and third dose of DPT iii. Attending growth monitoring and counseling sessions

The three installments and amounts have been worked out such that the beneficiary is due to receive a reasonable amount every three months after the second trimester of pregnancy up to six months after delivery (including the JSY tranche). Further, by linking the benefits to specific nutrition and health-related conditionalities that include the uptake of services offered through the Department of Health, IGMSY aims to

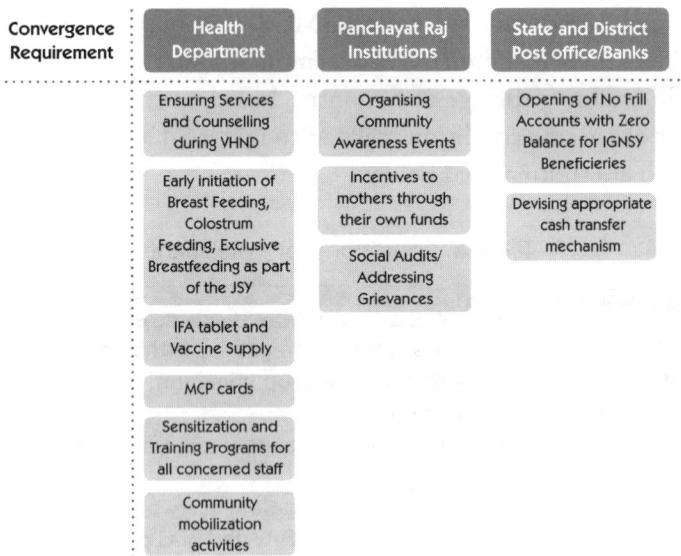

Figure 10.3: Convergence under the Scheme[3]

---

[3] Mapped on the basis of IGMSY Scheme Guidelines, 2011

also promote appropriate practices, care and service utilization during pregnancy, safe delivery and lactation; encourage women to follow (optimal) Infant and Young Child Feeding (IYCF) practices including early and exclusive breastfeeding for the first six months; and generally contribute to a better enabling environment by providing cash incentives for improved health and nutrition to pregnant and lactating women.

The Indira Gandhi Matritva Sahayog Yojana (IGMSY) utilizes the platform of the ICDS, the flagship program of the MWCD. As the figure below shows, the scheme guidelines require close coordination with the Department of Health and Panchayati Raj Institutions. Lead State and District Post Office/Banks are responsible for opening zero balance accounts for IGMSY beneficiaries and devising an appropriate cash transfer mechanism for smooth transactions in 52 selected districts.

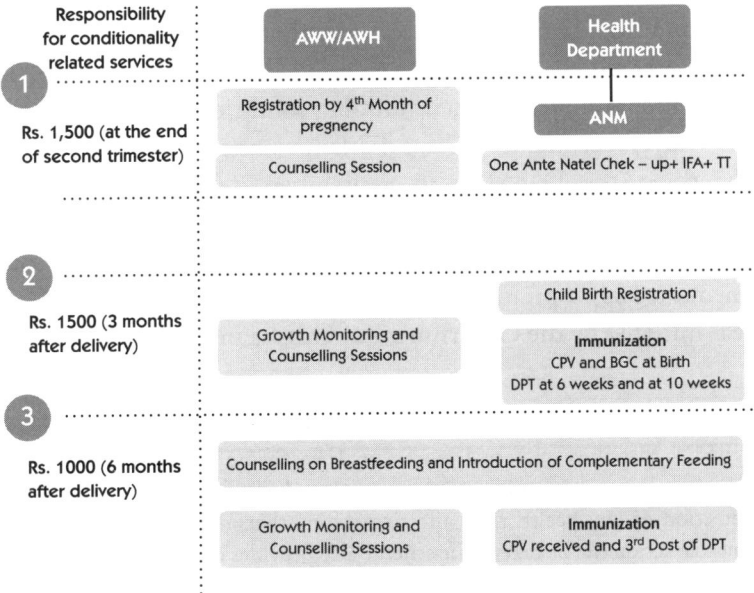

Figure 10.4: Responsibility for conditionality related services[4]

---

[4] Mapped on the basis of IGMSY Scheme Guidelines, 2011

The implementation machinery is yet to fully fall into place. Only a few states have set up dedicated IGMSY cells at the state and district levels. Delays in state government releases of funds received from the center, and the somewhat cumbersome procedure of approvals and bills submissions in order for cash benefits to be released appear to create significant time-delays of between one to two years in releases of funds for the scheme and payment of cash benefits. Monitoring remains weak across most states. Timely receipt of installments has proven to be a challenge, largely because of release of funds from state governments and hurdles in opening up zero balance bank accounts for beneficiaries.

Two comparable state-level schemes are Mamata in Odisha and Dr. Muthulakshmi Reddy Maternity Benefit Scheme (DMMBS) in Tamil Nadu.[5] There are some interesting commonalities and variations between the schemes. All three are conditional cash transfer schemes that track women through their pregnancy and lactation period and pay them cash in installments subject to their fulfilling conditionalities.

The Government of Tamil Nadu launched the oldest of the three, the DMMBS in September 2006 to compensate wage loss during pregnancy and lactation, incentivize positive health, increase institutional deliveries among poor families, and encourage appropriate practices amongst poor mothers. Mamata was initiated by the Government of Odisha in 2011 with the aim

---

[5] In 2012, Assam Government launched the "Mamoni Scheme" under NRHM to reduce maternal mortality. The scheme intends to encourage pregnant women to undergo three antenatal check-ups to enable early detection of any health risks affecting the mother and her foetus, so that suitable action can be taken. The scheme also provides every pregnant woman a booklet containing tips on safe motherhood and ways to care the new-born. The pregnant woman is given a small amount of Rs. 1,000 in the second and the third antenatal check-ups to enable her to meet expenses related to nutritional food and supplements.

of encouraging appropriate practices amongst poor pregnant and lactating mothers, increasing institutional deliveries among BPL families, compensating for wage loss during pregnancy and lactation, and incentivizing positive health practices.

Table 7: Comparison of Maternity Benefit Schemes—Installments and Conditionalities

	IGMSY	Mamata	Dr. Muthulakshmi Maternal Benefit Scheme (DMMBS)
Installment I – Benefit Payable (Time)	Rs. 1,500 At the end of second trimester	Rs. 1,500 At the end of second trimester	Rs. 4,000 Released in the seventh month of pregnancy
Installment I – Conditions	1. Registration of pregnancy at AWC / health center within four months of pregnancy	1. Registration of pregnancy at AWC/mini AWC.	1. At least three antenatal visits at the nearest PHC
	2. At least one antenatal check-up with IFA tablets and TT	2. At least one antenatal check-up with IFA tablets and TT	2. Have availed TT vaccine, blood grouping and typing, Hb level measurement, BP and weight check up, HIV test and ultra sonogram
	3. At least one counseling session at AWC/VHND	3. One counseling session at AWC or village Health and Nutrition day	

	IGMSY	Mamata	Dr. Muthulakshmi Maternal Benefit Scheme (DMMBS)
Installment II – Benefit Payable (Time)	Rs. 1,500 Three months after delivery	Rs. 1,500 Three months after delivery	Rs. 4,000 On delivery
Installment II – Conditions	1. Registered childbirth	1. Registered childbirth	1. Delivery has to be in a government institution.
	2. Child has received OPV and DPT	2. Immunization - BCG, DPT, Polio	
	3. At least two growth monitoring sessions and IYCF counseling during the three months after delivery	3. At least two growth monitoring and two IYCF counseling sessions at AWC/VHND/ Home Visits	
Installment III – Benefit Payable (Time)	Rs. 1,000 Six months after delivery	Rs. 1,000 Six months after delivery	Rs. 4,000 On completion of third dose of DPT/ Hepatitis B and Polio/Pentavalent vaccine for the child as per the time schedule.

	IGMSY	Mamata	Dr. Muthulakshmi Maternal Benefit Scheme (DMMBS)
Installment III – Conditions	1. If the child has been exclusively breast-fed for first six months, introduced to complementary food after that.	1. If the child has been exclusively breast-fed for first six months, introduced to complementary food after that.	
	2. Immunization - OPV and DPT	2. Immunization - OPV and DPT	
	3. At least two growth monitoring sessions and counseling sessions between three to six months	3. Atleast two IYCF counseling sessions between three to six month of lactation.	
Installment IV – Benefit	NA	Rs. 1,000	NA
Installment IV – Conditions	NA	Child has been weighed twice between six to nine months, given age specific complementary food, vitamin A first dose and measles vaccine before year one.	NA

The amount of benefit varies with IGMSY being the lowest at Rs. 4,000, Mamata at Rs. 5,000, and DMMBS being the highest at Rs. 12,000[6] per beneficiary. The provisions under DMMBS, and importantly, the recently approved Food Security Bill (2013)[7] also have implications for the amount of incentive. According to Section 4, Chapter II, detailing provisions for food security,

> Subject to such schemes as may be framed by the Central Government, every pregnant woman and lactating mother shall be entitled to –
> Clause (b) maternity benefit of not less than rupees six thousand, in such installments as may be prescribed by the Central Government:
> Provided that all pregnant women and lactating mothers in regular employment with the Central Government or State Governments or Public Sector Undertakings or those who are in receipt of similar benefits under any law for the time being in force shall not be entitled to benefits specified in clause (b).

Thus the minimum amount of maternity benefit should not be less than Rs. 6,000 where such schemes exist, according to this provision. These important benchmarks can serve to strengthen IGMSY as a unique maternity benefit scheme across the country, and make it more effective.

Perhaps the most important discussion has to be around the scheme's intended target group and prescriptions for eligibility. Eligibility criteria of the schemes are similar in terms of age

---

[6] The benefit under DMMBS was Rs. 6,000 until 2011. It was later revised and increased to Rs. 12,000.

[7] On 3 July 2013, the Union Cabinet approved to declare an ordinance on The National Food Security Bill (2013). On 5 July 2013, President Pranab Mukherjee signed and cleared the ordinance.

of beneficiary at 19 years, and up to two live births. Mamata and DMMBS are targeted towards poor women. In terms of conditionalities, Mamata has similar conditionalities for each installment compared to IGMSY; DMMBS differs in that it has fewer conditionalities for the second and third installments, restricting them to institutional deliveries at government institutions, and immunization of the infant, respectively. IGMSY also excludes women who are employees or spouses of employees of Government/Public Sector Undertakings (Central and State). The rationale behind laying these eligibility criteria is to reinforce that marriage and childbirth should occur only after the legal age of 18 years and to prevent repeated or numerous pregnancies (Scheme Guidelines). But we also know that according to the third National Family Health Survey (NFHS), every second woman in India is married before the legal age of 18 and every

Table 8: Women excluded by eligibility criteria (NFHS-3)

Category of Women	% of all women aged 15–49 who have given birth in the last year	Among women aged 15–49 who have given birth in the last year	
		Eligible by IGMSY criteria (%)	Ineligible by IGMSY criteria (%)
		(% of women aged 19–49 years having 2 or less than 2 births)	(% of women aged 15–49 years having more than 2 births)
All women	100	52	48
SC/ST/Poor having no education*	66	41	59
SC and ST	31	44	56
Poor Women	40	37	63
No Education	46	34	66

Source: Lingam and Yelamanchili 2011 (Computed from NFHS-3, 2005–06).
* Figures in categories overlap with more than one variable.

third woman aged 25–49 becomes a mother before the age of 18. An undernourished woman faces greater risk of obstructed labor, having a baby with low birth weight, adverse pregnancy outcomes, negative affects on lactation, death due to postpartum haemorrhage, and illness for herself and her baby.

Lingam and Yelamanchili (2011) have expressed concerns over the exclusionary criteria of the IGMSY scheme and using NFHS data, show the ways in which most vulnerable women get excluded from a benefit they sorely need. For instance, 48% women will be ineligible if exclusion criteria as per the IGMSY are adopted. 59% women having any one of the vulnerabilities in terms of caste, class or education will get left out. 56% of the Scheduled Caste/Scheduled Tribe, 63% of the poor and 66% of the uneducated women will fall out of the purview of this scheme.

Rural women, women belonging to SC/ST communities and lower socio-economic communities, with little to no education, and below 20 years of age show poor reproductive and maternal health outcomes. They have higher Total Fertility Rate (TFR), and higher Infant Mortality Rate (IMR) compared to those women eligible for the scheme. The requirement of a minimum age of 19 years to receive the benefit will serve to leave out substantive groups of marginalized women; at the same time, the criterion of a maximum of 'two live births' excludes 50% of SC/ST women, 58% poor women and 62% women with no education. While the government's assumption that inclusion of strict elibigility criteria around age and number of children in schemes like IGMSY will send a positive/corrective signal remains to be evaluated over time, they also signal particular trade-offs in policy decisions. There is enough evidence that early marriage and high fertility are consequences of deep-seated patriarchal values and social disadvantage based on gender – women have little control over fertility or decision-making in marriage.

Conclusion

The three frameworks are not meant to be water-tight—for instance IGMSY is meant for compensating wage loss for women in the informal sector (labor framework) and also ensuring uptake of ante- and post- natal services (health and nutrition framework)—but rather as analytical categories. Safe maternity requires achievements in women's rights to decent work and economic empowerment, as well as their access to quality health services and nutrition.

By way of an analysis, one may ask a range of questions. For instance, does it makes sense to have differential and, one might add, unequal entitlements for different groups such as for women in the formal sector who receive maternity benefits under the law, and those in the informal sector who receive them as conditional transfers. Even when a scheme like IGMSY makes the important provision for compensating for wage loss, by linking it to uptake of health services, it risks appearing to see women's right to a maternity benefit as an instrumental factor in reaching health targets. Further, while it is important to ensure access of benefits to women in the informal sector, the distinction between 'working' (for remuneration) and 'non-working' (in care work) may also seem problematic. At the same time, IGMSY may be a forerunner to other schemes by going beyond the poor/non-poor distinction by way of eligibility (albeit, its other eligibility criteria do exclude a vast number of women). In the insurance framework, the extension of the benefit as a household benefit rather than an individual one risks excluding women. Recognizing and extending individual entitlements to women seem more advantageous, at least in terms of recognition. The decision about when and where the women get covered is also something that seems to be adhocism in the scheme, but this can be easily addressed. However, the fact that RSBY is the only state insurance scheme that covers maternity deserves appreciation. Finally, the various approaches appear fragmented in a way that the experience of maternity for women is not. There is an urgent need to see how all of the current provisions fit and work together for women and the lived reality of maternity within familial, social, and economic contexts. Frameworks must be evolved that balance universal coverage with enough attention to, and provision for the particular, while recognizing the individual needs of different groups of women, gender norms and disparities, and economic and contextual realities.

REFERENCES

Berman, Peter et al. (2010), 'The Impoverishing Effect of Healthcare Payments in India: New Methodology and Findings', *Economic & Political Weekly*, Vol. XLV, No. 16. 17 April, pp. 65–71

Lingam, Lakshmi and Yelamanchili, Vaidehi (2011), 'Reproductive Rights and Exclusionary Wrongs: Maternity Benefits. Review of Women's Studies', *Economic & Political Weekly*, Vol. XLVI, No. 43. 22 October, pp. 94–103

MSPI (2004), *National Sample Survey 60th Round Report on Morbidity, Healthcare, and the Condition of the Aged*, New Delhi.

Mukherjee, S. et al. (2013), 'Maternity or catastrophe: A study of household expenditure on maternal health care in India', *Health*, Vol. 5, No. 1, pp. 109–18.

NCEUS (2007), *Report on Conditions of Work and the Promotion of Livelihoods in the Unorganized Sector*, New Delhi.

NSSO, India–Employment and Unemployment: NSS 61st round: July 2004–June 2005

Selvaraj, Sakthivel and Karan, Anup K. (2009), 'Deepening Health Insecurity in India: Evidence from National Sample Surveys since 1980s', *Economic & Political Weekly*, Vol. XLIV, No. 40. 3 October, pp. 55–60

UNICEF (2005), *2005 Coverage Evaluation Survey, All India Report*, New Delhi: UNICEF.

UNICEF (2008), *The State of the World's Children 2009: Maternal and Newborn Health*, New York: UNICEF.

UNICEF (2010), *2009 Coverage Evaluation Survey, All India Report*, New Delhi: UNICEF.

Strengthening NREGA from a Gender Perspective

Learnings from the field

SUBHALAKSHMI NANDI*

The Mahatma Gandhi National Rural Employment Guarantee Act (MGNREGA) was passed as an Act of Parliament in 2005 as a result of strong political will and due to a vibrant nation-wide movement of workers and farmers. In a country like India, with 93% of the workforce in informal employment, where 79% women workers in rural areas are in agriculture, and earn about 50–75% of the wages that men earn (Saxena, 2012), and of whom about 81% belong to marginalized communities (ILO, 2010), the right to guaranteed employment was bound to have huge implications. It was also a context in which large numbers of landless laborers were forced to survive on a daily wage rate of less than 0.80 USD. NREGA (later renamed the Mahatma Gandhi NREGA or MGNREGA) came with a promise of

---

* This paper was written with research support from Leena Patel and Suhela Khan, and reflects the learnings from a UN Fund for Gender Equality project 'Dalit Women's Livelihoods Accountability Initiative (DWLAI)', done in partnership with Gender at Work and its local partners in India.

guaranteeing 100 days of employment to a family within a range of five kilometers of their residence, based on written or spoken demand for work. Not only has MGNREGA created a legal and institutional basis for the right to work, rights at work, right to wage parity and minimum wage, backed by strong accountability mechanisms, it is also beginning to inspire a longer-term vision of reviving the agriculture sector through building assets for rural communities and supporting their livelihoods. It addresses poverty, deprivation and vulnerability by providing wage employment, creating assets, strengthening panchayats[1] and activating local mechanisms for social audit, thereby being both enabling and protective at the same time.

Table 1: Pro-Women Provisions in MGNREGA

One-third workers to be women
Equal pay for work of equal value
Provision of crèche facilities
Provision of work within 5 km radius of home

MGNREGA also offers a 'way out' for daily wage laborers from traditional feudal structures, which not only offer piecemeal wage rates but are intrinsically linked to class and caste-based discrimination, often 'bonded' forms of labor as well. Thus, the law is significant from a labor rights perspective particularly for women laborers, who belong to the most socio-economically marginalized communities, and who otherwise have no access to just employment opportunities. MGNREGA also provides workers with the opportunity to be part of governance structures—from implementation and monitoring oversights to ensuring administrative transparency and accountability,

---

[1] Constitutionally elected body that is the unit of the Indian three-tier system of local self-governance.

through the provision of social audits and the practice of appointing worksite supervisors ('mates').

There was already a precedence of an Employment Guarantee Scheme in the state of Maharashtra, which had been the outcome of a struggle for protection from poverty and unemployment that began during the massive drought of 1970–73. Maharashtra's Employment Guarantee Act (1979) provided guaranteed employment to all adults throughout the year in public works involving unskilled manual work with timely wage payment, and encouraged creation of productive assets. As guaranteed employment and universality were the cornerstone of this Act, it outlived governments and managed to address destitution by enabling survival and food security, brought about social inclusion, ensured institutional accountability and increased 'bargaining power' of the poor, especially of the most vulnerable such as women belonging to Scheduled Caste (SC) and Scheduled Tribe (ST) communities.

The national legislation was a departure from the universal right to employment, as the number of days was limited to 100, and what essentially is an individual right was dwindled down to a household entitlement, thereby becoming a barrier for women's participation in its very design. Nevertheless, within the larger context of rural poverty and feminization of poverty, MGNREGA continues to be the government's flagship program in fulfilling the right to work. It is the largest of its kind in the world, reaching out to an unprecedented number of rural poor, including women.

Issues Related to Women's Participation in MGNREGA

An extensive review of literature undertaken by the Ministry of Rural Development (MGNREGA Sameeksha Report, 2012), on studies related to MGNREGA, revealed that much of the work has been carried out in documenting women's participation and access to wage employment under MGNREGA. It has been well documented that women prefer to work under MGNREGA as opposed to other options since they can do so in the vicinity of their homes and enjoy decent work conditions. There is also some evidence of the growing wage parity between men and women, as well as of women's access and control over financial resources due to earnings from MGNREGA. By and large, however, while there is a lot of research examining the implementation of MGNREGA entitlements, there is very little work on understanding gender outcomes and structural issues in MGNREGA.

Lack of such data also fails to contribute to any analysis of regional disparities. While women's participation in the state of Kerala is as high as 94%, it is only 17% in the state of Uttar Pradesh (Government of India, 2011–12). The difference between states in the North and South can, to some extent, be explained by the longstanding institutional base of women in the South, mainly in the form of women's groups, which have enabled women to build on their collective strength and bargaining power to negotiate for decent work. Further, state support and initiatives such as the Kudumbashree program of Kerala, which has strong linkages with Panchayati Raj Institutions (PRIs), have also buoyed women's participation (Muraleedharan, 2012). Moreover, there could be other labor market dynamics contributing to regional disparities.

Anecdotal evidence from states like Uttar Pradesh (UP) suggested that women were discriminated against simply because the entitlement stipulated in MGNREGA is contingent on the household. This meant that women did not have the same opportunities in accessing MGNREGA as men. When seeking information about the law/scheme and seeking employment under MGNREGA, women were turned back with the message that they should 'come back with the men'. Not surprisingly, MGNREGA work (just like intra-household distribution of nutrition, education, assets and income) was initially prioritized for the 'primary breadwinner', i.e., men. Whether the individual, rather than the household, could be the unit of entitlement was not a question that policymakers or workers' movements took up, nor was it debated enough among feminists (Nandi, 2011). Later, this issue was taken up actively by single women's associations across the country and the MGNREGA guidelines for what constitutes a 'household' were subsequently redefined.

Moreover, women are not a homogenous group. Marginalized women are confronted with the triple hurdles of gender, class and caste in securing work under MGNREGA. For example, single and elderly women are marginalized because works are mostly allocated to couples or families through a group system. The physical nature of MGNREGA work also discriminates against breastfeeding mothers, elderly women, and those with disabilities. Sub-groups of Dalit women, such as Musahar[2] and Muslim women who are amongst the poorest, often find themselves completely out of the purview of MGNREGA. Lack of awareness about the Act, about its history, vision and provisions, sometimes makes MGNREGA seem like a 'dole' as opposed to a right.

Dalit Women's Livelihood Accountability Initiative (DWLAI): Grassroots Feminist Interventions

To address some of these gaps, UN Women's Fund for Gender Equality (FGE) supported the Dalit Women Livelihoods Accountability Initiative (DWLAI), a project that was undertaken with Dalit women of Andhra Pradesh (AP) and UP from 2010 to 2012, to include their perspective in

---

[2] One of the most marginalized Scheduled Caste communities of Northern India.

social accountability mechanisms as part of MGNREGA implementation. The project was implemented by Gender at Work, along with grassroots partner organizations in eight districts of AP and UP. This essay is based primarily on learnings and reflections from the UP experience of Gender at Work, which happened across 69 panchayats of 5 districts, and was implemented by four local organisations—Lok Samiti, Parmarth Sewa Sansthan, Sahajani Shiksha Kendra (SSK), and Vanangana. The project aimed at increasing Dalit women's participation and empowerment through MGNREGA, and employed a three-fold strategy of increasing access, participation and enhancing transparency and accountability. This project helped to demonstrate that where facilitated, women have actively accessed and participated meaningfully in MGNREGA, while being empowered socially, economically and politically (Ojha, 2012).

In UP, women's participation in MGNREGA has continuously remained below par. The geographical areas of the project intervention and state context is characterized as backward with high levels of impoverishment and marginalization, low social and economic indicators, and a physical climate and terrain which is dry, arid and harsh. Women's participation, especially Dalit women's participation is beleaguered with the same structural problems (identified in the earlier section) of caste, class and gender. In addition, women's engagement with PRIs, which is the key formal institution related to MGNREGA implementation, especially in planning and other decision-making processes, was negligible. Thus, the project sought to close the gap that existed between legislative guarantees and implementation at the ground level. A glimpse of the results achieved in the project is given below.

Table 2: Results from DWLAI (2010–12)

	Baseline (2010)				Endline (2012)			
Percentage of women accessing MGNREGA (%)	61.7				97			
Number of Days (%)	<25	26–50	51–75	>75	<25	26–50	51–75	>75
	87	8	2	3	5.9	24.3	57.3	12.5
Worksite Facilities (crèche) (%)	1.1				2.6			
Women worksite supervisors (Mates) (%)	1.2				20.74			
Individual Bank Accounts (%)	30				70			
Non-MGNREGA wages: agricultural work (figures in USD)	Women 0.8	Men 1.2			Women 1.3	Men 1.45		
Non-MGNREGA wages: non-farm work (figures in USD)	Women 0.9	Men 1.6			Women 1.6	Men 1.9		

Some initiatives were piloted to promote the participation and leadership of women under MGNREGA, as workers, mates (worksite supervisors), and as community leaders, working closely with PRIs. For instance, Lok Samiti's project aimed at enabling access to MNREGA of Musahar and Muslim women by getting women from these communities Job Cards and work for the first time since the implementation of the Act, and enabled their participation in mainstream workers' unions. This initiative also sought to break gender and community-based barriers and stereotypes (e.g., the perception that Muslim women are not interested or allowed to do manual work). Sahajani Shiksha Kendra trained Dalit women to become 'mates'. For this they developed a training module specifically targeted at semi-literate women. The module combined perspective building with skill development and has been used to advocate for policy-level interventions to bring more women into these positions. This model challenged stereotypes related to women's abilities to do 'technical' work. Vanangana initiated an all-women's work site—building a large pond—where Dalit women were involved in all stages of planning and implementing the work. This model helped to reduce barriers related to women's access to panchayats, and government departments, while enabling women as capable managers and decision-makers at a large worksite.

The first achievement of the project was **increase in employment and incomes** for women, both through access to employment under MGNREGA as well as through increase in the number of days of work they got. As Table 2 shows, 13% women managed to secure MGNREGA work for more than 75 days as compared to 3% in the baseline. Almost 77% women surveyed felt that there has been an improvement in their economic condition, as they have secured more working days. A large percentage of these women said they now spent their money to avoid hunger, repay small debts, and paying for their child's education. The second area of accomplishment was the **greater access to and control over financial resources** that women now enjoyed. As much as 70% of women managed to get a bank account in their name as compared to 30% in the baseline. More significantly, 72.4% of these women are now operating bank accounts on their own as compared to 53% in the baseline. Access to economic resources also had a favorable impact on women's say in household-decision-making. As many as 98% women said they now played a larger role in deciding how this money would be used. The project also helped women **trump gender stereotypes** since it gave them the opportunity to carry out semi-skilled and skilled work. Over the project period, about 150 women across all the project sites were trained as worksite supervisors (mates). The number of women who have worked as mates has increased from 1.2% to 21% during the project period, and women also gained confidence as a result of doing this work. They learnt to do technical tasks such as measurement of works, filling of 'muster rolls' (attendance registers), etc., which had traditionally been the domain of powerful men. Clearly, wages in rural areas have increased as a result of these changes. Data from the project (refer to Table 2) shows that there was a rise in wages in non-MGNREGA work, both in agriculture and non-farm sectors, and there was also a clear decline in the gender gap in wages. All these shifts signal changes in the lives of the women, and are indicative of their 'empowerment journeys' by challenging dominant power structures of gender, caste and class (Patel, Nandi and Khan 2012).

A joint advocacy consultation in December 2012 by UN Women and Gender at Work, showcasing and highlighting the learnings from this project, contributed to the adoption of policy recommendations, such as appointment of 50% women mates for all worksites, identification of single women for issuing individual Job Cards, and conduction of time studies motion studies to formulate schedule of rates (SOR) that are gender, age and disability sensitive. These provisions have now formally become part of the MGNREGA guidelines. On the invitation of the Central Ministry, UN Women in now supporting Rural Development Departments in four states that are still below the mandated 33% women's participation (Odisha, Jammu & Kashmir, Uttar Pradesh and West Bengal) in order to replicate some of these effective models to raise women's participation and ensure their rights.

On looking back at the experience, the strategies that were found most effective in achieving these results may be listed as follows:

- **Organizing women** for action, through peer learning, collectivising for building voice and agency, enhancing their bargaining power and developing solidarity. This provided a strong platform for women in public spaces and increased their negotiating power vis-à-vis family, community, landlords, banks, PRIs, and the government machinery.
- **Awareness and capacity-building** of all women in the project area on rights-based approaches, on the law and its provisions and of the process and cycle of MGNREGA right from developing work plans in Gram Sabhas till the payment of wages. In this project, capacity-building also included technical skill training for women and helping women obtain formal appointments as mates. The unique combination of perspective-based training on gender, caste and poverty, accompanied by technical and legal training, was a key strategy that sets this project apart from other capacity-building efforts.
- **Partnerships and alliance-building** was another key feature of this project, whether at the local community level or across the four partner organizations, or alliances with key leaders in the community, PRIs, government, and even among fellow activists.
- **Campaigns and advocacy** efforts were another key feature that led to the success of these programs, at the local level, and ultimately contributed to recognition and acknowledgment at the state and national levels, by bringing together a mixture of grassroots women and activists, non-government organizations, academicians, practitioners, donors, and the government.

LEARNINGS AND REFLECTIONS: A FEMINIST VISION OF RIGHTS AND EMPOWERMENT

There is no doubt that MGNREGA is a successful social protection measure for the most marginalized and excluded. Within the existing political economy, the passing of the law was a huge battle in itself, and so is its day-to-day implementation. Yet, from the perspective of its gender-responsiveness, the learnings from the DWLAI suggest the mere enactment of law is not enough. A bottom-up paradigm, with **both rights-based approaches and empowerment processes at its core**, is needed for the desired outcomes for gender equality to become a reality. An important element of the gender perspective in a human rights framework is the centrality of 'empowerment' processes. In the literature in recent years, 'rights-based approaches' and 'empowerment approaches' have often been pitted against each other. Part of the reason for this is that the interpretation of these frameworks has been appropriated by players other than those who created the discourse (Cornwall, 2007). Nevertheless, for gender equality advocates, 'empowerment' remains a critical framework, at the core of which is an analysis of power. Empowerment is defined as the process, and the outcome of the process, by which women gain greater control over material and intellectual resources, and challenge the ideology of patriarchy and gender-based discrimination of women in all institutions and structures of society (Batliwala, 2013).

From a gender perspective, therefore, the learning is that rights and empowerment complement each other. While rights are the 'the value framework that guides intervention', empowerment provides the 'nuts and bolts for organizing communities, particularly those with poor women, around these values and ideas' (Kapur and Duvvury, 2005). The DWLAI provides one example of how feminist organizing on the ground (empowerment) within the framework of the law (rights) helped women not only in accessing their entitlements under MGNREGA but was also instrumental in helping them challenge other institutions and sources of marginalization such as caste, class and literacy.

An important reflection from the grassroots feminist interventions in DWLAI is that further investments in empowerment—for organizing women, building their networks and institutions, dialoging with social movements, and increasing their voice and agency—have to urgently become part of the discourse on social protection in India. In keeping with the CEDAW[3] principle of state obligation, and in line with India's own constitutional framework, there is a clear role to be played by the government for provisioning, budgeting and tracking of outcomes of social protection policies and schemes, including the creation of appropriate monitoring and grievance redressal mechanisms that engage people, especially women, from marginalized communities in substantive roles. The DWLAI experience reminds us that in addition to a rights-based approach, empowerment and transformation should once again become a central agenda in the discourse, organizing and strategizing for social protection in India.

REFERENCES

Batliwala, Srilatha (2013), 'Engaging with empowerment: An intellectual and experiential journey', New Delhi: Women Unlimited.

Cornwall, Andrea (2007), 'Buzzwords and fuzzwords: Deconstructing development discourse', in *Development in Practice*, Vol. 17, No. 4–5; viewed on 17 June 2013 (http://my.ewb.ca/site_media/static/attachments/threadedcomments_threadedcomment/56066/25901768.pdf)

Government of India, MGNREGA National Reports 2006–10, Ministry of Rural Development (MoRD). Viewed on 30 April 2013 (http://nrega.nic.in/netnrega/home.aspx)

International Labour Organization (2010), 'Women workers in agriculture: Expanding responsibilities and shrinking opportunities', New Delhi: International Labour Organization

---

[3] CEDAW: Convention on the Elimination of All Forms of Discrimination against Women.

Jones, Nicola (2012), 'Women's empowerment—The role of social protection'. Paper presented at an Expert Group Meeting on Social Protection in South East Asia.

Kapur, Aanchal and Duvvury, Nata (2005), 'A rights-based approach to realising the economic and social rights of poor and marginalised women: A synthesis of lessons learned', New Delhi: International Center for Research on Women. Viewed on 17 June 2013 (http://www.icrw.org/files/publications/A-Rights-Based-Approach-to-Realizaing-the-Economic-and-Social-Rights-of-Poor-and-Marginalized-Women.pdf)

Muraleedharan, Sarada (2012), 'MGNREGS and Kerala—The untold story'. Viewed on 1 May 2013 (ftp://ftp.solutionexchange.net.in/public/gen/cr/res22031301.pdf)

Nandi, Subhalakshmi (2011), 'Feminist engagement with the "body" and "labour" within "mainstream" development discourse'. Paper presented at XIII Indian Association for Women's Studies Conference at Wardha.

National Human Rights Commission (NHRC, 2011), 'Know your rights: The Right to Work'. Available at http://www.nhrc.nic.in/Documents/Publications/KYR%20Work%20English.pdf; accessed on 22 January 2014.

Ojha, Gana Pati (2012), 'Evaluation of UN Women Fund for Gender Equality Economic and Political Empowerment Catalytic Grant Program, "Dalit Women's Livelihoods Accountability Initiative", India'. Viewed on 18 June 2013 (http://www.unwomen.org/wp-content/uploads/2012/05/FGE-Programme-Evaluation-Gender-at-Work-DSS-India-2012-EN.pdf)

Patel, Leena, Nandi, Subhalakshmi and Khan, Suhela (2012), 'Women's labour rights in a globalising world—Insights from the field'. Paper presented at the 54th Annual Conference of the Indian Society of Labour Economics (ISLE).

Right to Food Campaign: 'A Brief on the Right to Work'. Available at http://www.righttofoodindia.org/rtowork/rtw_briefing.pdf; accessed on 22 January 2014

Saxena, N. C. (2012), 'Women, land and agriculture in rural India', UN Women. Viewed on 16 June 2013 (http://www.

unwomensouthasia.org/assets/UN_Women_Land_Agriculture_ in_Rural_India.pdf)

Sepúlveda, Magdalena and Nyst, Carly (2012), 'The human rights approach to social protection', Ministry of Foreign Affairs, Government of Finland.

Women and Social Security

Convergence model of delivery

RASHMI SINGH

Social security programs for women, besides addressing the need for a safety net, also enhance the productive capacity of women and create a level-playing field. This is more critical in the case of women where there are inherent socio-eco-cultural barriers, which prevent them from equal access to opportunities as men. In order to reduce the vulnerability of women, it is also important that a life-cycle approach be adopted where all stages of girls'/ women's lives are seen as a continuum where inputs at every stage have an impact on the growth and development at another stage. Further, the women's needs cannot be seen in segments, since the responses related to heath, physical well-being, education, skill, employment, safety and security, etc., are closely related to one another. This sets the context for adopting a convergent mode of delivery for ensuring women's social security.

SOCIAL SECURITY IN INDIA

Traditionally, the family has been the informal social security system in India. Joint families have largely been the norm, with members taking responsibility for those in need. The social safety net has hence traditionally been provided by the joint/extended family support system. India being primarily an agrarian country, the access/ownership of material assets like land and livestock, ensured a minimum security for even those who may not directly be productive members of the family and community. In keeping with cultural traditions, family members and relatives displayed a spirit of shared responsibility towards one another.

However, with increasing migration, urbanization, and diversification of economy, large, joint families have become fewer, and nuclear families more prevalent. This has created a greater need for having a formal and institutionalized system of social security for those in need of care and protection.

Women's Vulnerability

Given the multiple vulnerabilities and gender-based discrimination, which women face and are prone to, a more focussed approach and multi-pronged intervention in this regard is clearly needed. Women's vulnerabilities begin with a struggle for the right to life, as is evident from the unfortunate practice of female foeticide. Women are also vulnerable because of malnutrition due to poverty and discrimination, discrimination in education, limited property rights, control on resources, participation in decision-making, issues related with legal rights, atrocities, rape, trafficking, health and HIV/AIDS, child marriage, domestic violence, violence in society, etc., apart from exploitation within the family at different stages. Further, it is universally accepted that women's vulnerabilities are age-related. In early childhood, girls are vulnerable for physical survival whilst adolescent and married women joust with a different set of vulnerabilities. Similarly, girls/women are also vulnerable to sexual abuses. Old age brings economic vulnerability whilst widowhood brings a variety of vulnerabilities depending upon the age at which the woman has become a widow. The web of vulnerability that arises due to deprivation has to be unbundled if we want to address the issue of inclusive development of women.

Given the above context and the complexity of the issues, the government faces the challenge of developing a comprehensive approach and institutional mechanism to prevent deprivation, assure minimum income and protect women from risks and uncertainties. The state bears the primary responsibility for developing an appropriate system for providing protection and minimum support system to its citizens.

It has been observed that most social security measures have been limited to the organized sectors. However, a large percentage of women in the workforce are in the unorganized sector. A majority of women in the labor force are engaged in unskilled, casual and seasonal jobs, which are low paid and lack social security cover.

The government has introduced various proactive legislations to provide social security cover from time to time, such as the Workmen's Compensation Act, 1923; Maternity Benefit Act, 1961; Employment State Insurance Scheme, 1948; Employees Provident Fund Act, 1952; and the Health Safety and Welfare of the Workers. In addition, laws have also been enacted to secure the interests of special categories. Also recently, the Supreme Court of India has given a landmark judgment protecting women against sexual harassment in the workplace.

A number of schemes have also been provided to meet the needs of special vulnerable categories such as old persons through the Old Age Pension Scheme, The Family Pension Scheme, 1964, Employment State Insurance Scheme, 1948, Employment Provident Fund Scheme, 1925, Coal Mines Provident Fund Bonus Scheme, 1948, and so on.

The present challenge lies in the enforceability of these acts and the effective implementation of the relevant schemes. At present there are numerous schemes that have been designed to provide social security and protection but they are fragmented and scattered across departments and ministries, i.e., both across horizontals and verticals. The challenge also lies in redressing the lack of awareness about the existing provisions of the acts and the procedural formalities involved with various schemes.

The Eleventh Five-Year Plan aimed at inclusive development with a vision that women are given an opportunity to develop their full potential and share the benefits of economic growth and prosperity. The plan period saw the introduction of many new schemes and programs targetted at specific groups and aimed at addressing specific issues. These included SABLA for empowering adolescent girls, Indira Gandhi Matritva Sahyog Yojana (IGMSY) for providing maternity benefits while complying to a set of conditionalities, Mahila Kisan Sashaktikaran Yojana for women farmers, a scheme for leadership training of Minority women, Ujjawala for combating trafficking, and Dhanalakshmi to tackle the issue of declining sex ratio, apart from the National Mission for Empowerment of Women (NMEW).

The Convergence Model and Social Security of Women

Given the multitude of schemes, and the concomitant absence of a comprehensive social protection scheme, maximum impact can only be felt through a convergent mode of delivery, starting from measures for convergence at the level of planning and implementation. There has been an increasing recognition that concrete measures are needed to create synergies for improving the quality of outcomes. It has been understood that in order to address women's needs holistically and across sectors, not only is the design and delivery of a program important but also how the inter-linkages are conceptualized at the outset.

The Twelfth Five-Year Plan recognizes that interventions in

favor of women must be multi-pronged and they must provide women with basic entitlements, address the need for socio-economic empowerment, ensure an environment free from all forms of violence against women, ensure the participation and adequate representation of women in decision-making positions, and strengthen institutional mechanisms for gender mainstreaming in all policies and programs.

There is also a recognition that women are not a homogenous group. The status of women is affected by varying levels of deprivation and vulnerability and hence, the inter-sectionality of issues needs to be addressed. For instance, SC/ST women, women with HIV/AIDS, elderly women, women with chronic illness, and disabled women are prone to a greater degree of vulnerability and social exclusion. It is hence important to map and address the specific deprivations faced by these groups for effective planning and implementation of our schemes, programs and services. Coupled with general program interventions, special targetted interventions catering to the differential needs of special groups of women need to be taken on board.

The challenge also lies in addressing the life cycle needs of women, and respond to the need for multidisciplinary actions through multipronged efforts. Social exclusion has been exacerbated due to a lack of or limited access to public services and schemes to the most needy; effectiveness of existing social security schemes not being of the desired level; a lack of unified mechanisms for delivery; and programs being driven by a top-down approach rather than a bottom-up one.

It is being increasingly acknowledged that the lack of inter-sectoral convergence is a huge challenge to deriving maximum benefits from the resources already allocated for different schemes, programs, and services across ministries at the center and departments at the state level. Convergence measures are hence being adopted through conscious efforts in-built in schemes design as well as mechanisms which cut across different schemes.

In the overall social security framework for women, the focus has been on combining preventive along with remedial measures with the goal of empowering women and addressing their multiple needs. Convergence can be orchestrated in different forms. Programmatic convergence attempts to create horizontal linkages between various programs. For example, legal awareness for women is implemented by legal service authorities. Once the same is synergized with institutions created for women by the Department of Social Welfare and Ministry of Women and Child Development (MWCD), it leads to more effective delivery and improved outreach. The inclusion of Anganwadi construction among the schedule of works under NREGA is again an example of programmatic convergence.

Thematic convergence in turn sees the response addressing the different sectors together, for example, while addressing the need for skill training there is a simultaneous effort to improve literacy levels and the health status of the same target group. Institutions play a very important role in making such convergence efforts possible. These institutional mechanisms can manifest themselves in either co-location of services or single-window facilitation points through which access can be improved to different services spread across different service providers. The single-window approach minimizes the time and energy required on the part of those entitled to access social security measures. Such centres have to support the completion of documentary requirements such as getting the death certificate of the husband in case a widow has to apply for widow pension, or the proof of age for old age pension. At the same time, as a policy measure, documentary requirements have to be made very simple since the cumbersome procedures and formalities often keep the neediest away from even trying to avail many of the existing social security measures.

Mechanisms are needed to foster and strengthen convergence at all levels—the level of planning, service delivery and governance cutting across central, state, district, block and village levels. Administrative reforms are needed to bring greater structural alignment between existing structures. The reforms must start with the admission that only a holistic approach through synergistic efforts can make a difference. It must be acknowledged that issues such as violence against women is the result of several factors combined together and hence needs to be addressed with a macro view. The need to work across departmental boundaries and transcending the straightjacket approach gets recognized when issues get addressed via an interdepartmental effort. From the client's point of view needs are seen not in compartments but as a continuum where the inputs in one aspect will affect the output in some other aspect. For example, the health-seeking behavior of women will improve if they are more literate. Rationalization of schemes is another need of the moment, especially within the department by clubbing schemes with same or similar objectives which have had less impact on their own due to low unit cost and high transaction costs.

While at the conceptual levels the planning happens at the highest strata of policy-making bodies, the planning for convergence becomes pragmatic only when it is accompanied by a decentralized process, where the nuts and bolts of convergence get stitched together by units closer to the grassroots. For example, the Anganwadi workers, ashas, shikshamitra, panchayats are aware how the mechanism works on the ground in terms of synergistic working and optimum use of resources coming from different schemes and departments. Mechanisms still need to be created for participation, accountability and monitoring. Capacities of communities also have to built up so they can demand their rights and entitlements, and they have to be equipped with tools, which will help them seek accountability and effective participation.

Building up gender focal points and an inter-departmental coordination mechanism manifests itself through government orders, notifications, etc. For example, setting up the Inter-Departmental Coordinating Committee headed by the Chief Secretary with other relevant line departments can address women's holistic needs for social security more effectively. Similarly, constituting district co-ordination committees/ district convergence forums at the district levels under the district collector to bring together district-level nodal officers belonging to different department to address gender needs is an important institutional mechanism for convergent delivery of schemes and services. Regular meetings of such bodies are important to review the progress on issues of convergence.

The Case of Mission Convergence, Delhi and National Mission for Empowerment of Women

There are two programs—one at the state level and the other at the national level, where most of the strategies and approaches discussed in the above sections have been tried and tested with a reasonable amount of success. One relates to the Delhi Mission Convergence Program and the other is the National Mission for Empowerment of Women (NMEW) rolled out by the central government. In both, a combination of approaches for convergence with the ultimate goal of women's empowerment have been used with a focus on building capacities of the vulnerable and marginalized.

Mission Convergence was a response to the challenge of governing one of the fastest growing metropolitan cities with 14 million people (as per Census 2001) residing in slums and unauthorized colonies, and about 1,00,000 people reported as homeless. The need was felt for a participatory model of governance involving government and civil society. Foundations for this model had been laid in the past through the project 'Stree Shakti' under which a series of camps were organized in less-developed areas of Delhi with a concentration of women from low-income groups. These camps were organized by the Department of Social Welfare in active collaboration with NGOs. A number of stakeholders from different government departments and non-government organizations were engaged in a collaborative exercise. Women from a radius of 3–4 kilometers were pre-registered by community facilitators engaged by the local NGO and their needs mapped in terms of required interventions related primarily to their health, and accessing other schemes and services. During the camp, women were organized to avail the services provided by multiple service prodders from the same location. A folder called the Stree-Shakti card was maintained for each woman.

While the camp resulted in touching the lives of many women who were otherwise not on the radar of government schemes and services, with health as the entry point to reduce their vulnerability, it also paved the way for a more long-term sustainable model of setting up a network of centers at fixed locations close to Gender Resource Centres. A well-designed innovative program called Mission Convergence was created with a dedicated institutional mechanism to ensure effective and efficient delivery. An autonomous body Samajik Suvidha Sangam was created within the Government of National Capital Territory of Delhi (GNCTD) with the objective to develop convergence mechanisms for facilitating the access of different schemes and services of the government, and to minimize leakages and administrative costs by avoiding duplication and smoothening the outreach process.

The Mission Convergence became an innovative model of the GNCTD aiming at restructuring its governance architecture by providing convergence platforms for facilitating the delivery of multiple/cross-sectoral developmental schemes of the government. The Mission's focus has been on women so that through women the whole family could be reached more effectively.

In order to overcome the limitations of using income criteria for measuring household poverty, Mission Convergence developed a vulnerability criteria, which turned out to be a much more effective measure of urban poverty and vulnerability in Delhi. The criteria responded to the challenge of addressing the needs of migrants in Delhi. As a result, a vulnerability database emerged, which became the backbone of other interventions related to the poor and needy.

The Mission Convergence initiative was a move away from the traditional bureaucratic forms of governance by creating a fast track decision-making process and service-delivery platform. The mission effectively used IT tools and infrastructure for streamlining information related with eligibility and access across different schemes meant to serve the same target group. Mission Convergence's monitoring and evaluation system was strengthened by the involvement of mother NGOs in monitoring the activities of Gender Resource Center (GRC) Suvidha Kendras (SK) and third party audits and evaluations from time to time.[1]

The program cut across multiple areas of activity across sectors in contrast to the conventional approach of the government for social service delivery through the departmental mode, moving through vertical channels across nine departments, and a poor presence at the level of service delivery. One of the biggest strengths of this initiative has been the structured partnerships with NGOs with clear roles and responsibilities to match the strengths of the government machinery with community-based organizations.

---

[1] A system was put in place in the program for performance audit of all NGOs against defined targets. This was done through concurrent monitoring and evaluation through a mother NGO that would undertake regular field visits to oversee the activities being undertaken by the filed NGOs. Over and above, a third party audit was commissioned on an annual basis to evaluate the work of the field NGOs and the MNGOs.

Convergence platforms convened by the chief secretary, district collector (DC) or at the community level with GRC-Suvidha Kendra as the hub enhanced demand across different developmental schemes of the government through enhanced awareness levels and improved access, especially to those who were unreachable through regular facilitation support. For instance, the Rashtriya Swasthya Bima Yojna (RSBY) and Swarna Jayanti Shahari Rozgar Yojana (SJSRY), schemes once made to ride on the outreach provided by the GRCs, could be made to reach a larger spread than what was possible through the departmental channel of respective departments.

Identity documents through enrolment in Aadhaar, voter I-cards, and financial inclusion by opening bank accounts also made the process of availing various cash transfer programs like old age pension and widow pension more streamlined.

What makes it a unique initiative is a good mix of social security, and access to opportunities by creating a level playing field. The use of vulnerability criteria; registration and enrolment process through community-level mapping of vulnerable groups; and moving for budgetary allocation across schemes based on evidence such as gender disaggregated data are some strategies which made the design respond better to the needs of vulnerable women including the most marginalized, like homeless women.

Many of the elements of this model were incorporated by the Government of India in the new criteria for identification of urban poor by the committee constituted by the Planning Commission.

The NMEW was launched on 8 March 2010 by the Government of India with the aim to strengthen the overall process that promotes the all-round development of women and position women's concerns at the core of public policy and governance. It has the mandate to strengthen inter-sector convergence and facilitate the process of coordinating all women's welfare and socio-economic development programs across ministries and departments, enabling it to become a unified programmatic response cutting across sectors and to address some of the deeply entrenched structural and institutional biases that women experience.

The three levels at which the NMEW transacted are at the policy level through inter-ministerial/coordinated strategies cutting across sectors, convergence institutional mechanisms at the level of delivery systems, and through convergence platforms at the community level. Intervention at the policy level required a review of programs/schemes using the gender lens. Towards strengthening the implementation and delivery mechanism of the government schemes/programs and to empower women in a holistic manner, a network of convergence-cum-facilitation centers under the name of Poorna Shakti Kendras have been created across states. These Convergence centers work to bring greater awareness about women-based schemes and programs of the government, augment the demand for various services/schemes for women, and facilitate their linkages with different service providers, i.e., existing government machinery across different departments/ministries.

Recognizing the gap between policy, program design and delivery, the NMEW set up the appropriate institutional framework for facilitating coordinated and effective service delivery to women at the grassroots level.

The NMEW created a pan-Indian presence with outreach to most states/UTs through the formation of State Mission Authorities (SMAs) under the respective chief ministers with dedicated technical units called State Resource Centres for Women (SRCW) to carry on the day-to-day work. These structures are provided regular handholding and technical support from the Mission team at the center through a technical body comprising gender experts from different specializations relevant to women's needs such as poverty alleviation, health and nutrition, legal rights, education, gender budgeting, media and communication, IT, etc. This body is called the National Resource Center for Women and its uniqueness lies in being a multi-disciplinary body, which can address the needs of women in a more holistic manner than any single target program.

While the MWCD is the nodal ministry at the center and state-level for this Mission, various other ministries are provided with a common platform to address women's issues holistically, recognizing that gender issues are cross-cutting in nature.

The initiative presents an opportunity to demonstrate and scale up models for ensuring women's participation through single-window convergence-cum-facilitation centers called Poorna Shakti Kendras, and social mobilization programs like the Nari Ki Chaupal and Betijanamotsav successfully tested on ground as a part of this initiative. Women who are enrolled in the program through the convergence centers are linked with different programs of the government and also made more aware about the acts which affect them. These centers generate awareness on schemes and laws related to women, provide linkages to different government programs, reduce the gap between the government and community, and forge a collaborative relationship between the government and NGOs to collectively address issues related to women and the girl child.

Recognizing the need for convergence platforms at different levels, district facilitation and convergence centers have been created in some districts to start with and provided with outreach structures at the block and gram panchayat levels. These structures act as single-window facilitation-cum-service centers for women. Elected women representatives are provided training to improve their leadership skills, community awareness programs like Nari Ki Chaupal are organized from time to time, and innovative convergence projects on different themes are taken up to demonstrate processes, which can address different types of vulnerability related to women, such as witch-hunting, devdasis, child marriage, and so on. Studies/research and assessments into different areas of vulnerability related to caste, and gender-based discrimination with multiple layers of exclusion such as those related to groups like sex workers, women affected with HIV/AIDS/single women, etc., are also taken up.

Village-level coordinators engaged under the project are trained to act as social ambassadors. The program has shown very encouraging results since thousands of women's lives have already been touched through its various community-based interventions like stopping child marriage, enrolling girls in school, counselling against alcoholism and domestic violence, awareness against sex discrimination and female foeticide, linking women to government schemes like pensions, ICDS, Sabla, etc. Self-help groups of women/mahila mandals/other forms of women's collectives play an important role in acting as convergence platforms with greater leveraging capacities than individual women.

In the theme-based interventions using the convergence approach, some aspects being covered involve designing a social inclusion plan for socially marginalized and excluded populations with the aim to design and evolve processes to ensure that the basic entitlements and services for trafficked sex workers and transgender women are delivered consistently and on scale through better convergence and integration of various welfare schemes of the government.

The program has been working towards generating gender-disaggregated data about the socio-economic, political and demographic status of women through available secondary sources. This is in response to the need to understand the status of women across states/districts, and facilitate engagement with relevant issues, evolving gender-friendly initiatives, and taking pertinent policy decisions.

Sustained efforts are also made at various levels of governance with the objective of engendering the policies and programs of the government and of the local bodies, and for pursuing Gender Responsive Budgeting (GRB).

Policy-level discourses are also taken up to reduce the vulnerability of women, such as the valuation of the contribution of women engaged in household chores. The issue of unrecognized and unpaid work by women within their households has been the subject of an important debate for some time now. With the involvement of a wide section of stakeholders, such as economists, gender experts and representatives from other relevant ministries the need for focussed intervention towards recognition of work undertaken by women in the National Statistics and steps towards drudgery reduction for women engaged in unpaid household work have been worked out. The roadmaps spelt out the need for time-use surveys on a periodic basis. It was also recommended that the National Income Division of the Ministry of Statistics and Program Implementation and the MWCD should work together in the task of valuation of non-SNA work.

The NMEW program recognized the issue of declining Child Sex Ratio (CSR) as one of the major indicators of women disempowerment and undertook various steps at different levels to address this issue in a systemic manner. A multi-pronged and inter-sectoral approach was crystallized on the issue of CSR to ensure coordination between the various ministries and departments of the government. In this regard, the Ministry of Health & Family Welfare committed to improving the sex ratio at birth and reducing the gender differential in under-five child mortality. Specific targets were setup at the national and state level for the same. For effective implementation of the PCPNDT Act, the ministry is reviewing and developing guidelines/codes of conduct for states for various authorities under the act. The Ministry of Panchayati Raj (MoPR) issued an advisory to the Gram Panchayats to address the issue of declining CSR and creating awareness about valuing the girl child through Special Gram Sabha and Mahila Sabha action. A Thematic Convergence Project for improving CSR was undertaken in 10 selected districts of five states in partnership with MoPR. The Ministry of Labour & Employment agreed to undertake advocacy and awareness programs for addressing the issue of the declining CSR through the Central Board of Worker's Education (CBWE). In this regard a module has been developed by CBWE for its training programs to generate awareness among their workers on the issue. The Ministry of Drinking Water & Sanitation issued an advisory to states that 'Swachhata Doots' (Sanitation Messengers) shall help create awareness about the CSR and women's empowerment issues. The Ministry of Human Resource Development agreed to effectively implement guidelines/protocols for girl child-friendly schools, especially in 100 gender-critical districts. The Department of Legal Affairs under the Ministry of Law & Justice agreed to provide legal counseling/aid/awareness on PCPNDT Act and other legislations using state/district/taluka structures of the National Legal Services Authority (NALSA). This was an outcome of a series of inter-ministerial dialogues and consultations convened by the Secretary, MWCD, and facilitated by the team of experts engaged in the National Resource Centre for Women during the period 2013–14.

Conclusion

The convergence model has proved its relevance as an efficient approach at the policy level and effective delivery mechanism for social protection in both rural and urban settings. Convergence platforms, whether in the form of Delhi's Gender Resource Centers or Rajasthan's Poorna Shakti Kendra, act as magnets where various programmatic interventions can converge on the target group.

Some of the common strategies informing the convergent

approach are micro-planning using sex-disaggregated data; aligning existing structures of line departments to ensure synergy between resources; and pushing for a bottom-up approach with centralized planning, coupled with local ownership and community resource centers.

The biggest learning from the convergence model has been that when women become prime movers for their own development, and are supported with women-oriented centers/focal points, their vulnerability reduces and their access to various services—education, skill training, livelihood linkages, health services—improves, as does their awareness regarding social issues and their decision-making power.

About the Editor and Contributors

EDITOR

Priti Darooka is the founder and executive director of the Programme on Women's Economic, Social and Cultural Rights (PWESCR). She works in partnership with diverse groups and networks to provide support, and is part of several initiatives on women's poverty, right to livelihoods including right to land, social security and right to food. She strives to make human rights frameworks and mechanisms relevant to address issues of poverty.

CONTRIBUTORS

Aasha Kapur Mehta works with the Indian Institute of Public Administration, New Delhi. Her work focuses on concerns like poverty, deprivation, disparities and issues of vulnerable groups.

Anjor Bhaskar is a visiting research fellow at the Institute for Human Development, Eastern Regional Centre, and works on issues of sustainable development. He has been engaged in grassroots organization, activism and action research, mostly around NREGA, social security and waste management. He has recently co-authored a book on the impact of wells constructed under NREGA in Jharkhand, titled *All's Well That Ends in a Well*.

Biraj Patnaik is the principal advisor to the Supreme Court of India commissioners on the right to food. He was closely associated with the processes of drafting and lobbying for the National Food Security Act. He is the founder-member and on the board of several organizations, including State Health Resource Center, Public Health Resource Center, Centre for Equity Studies, Mobile Creches and Amnesty International India.

Dr. N.C. Saxena is an Indian bureaucrat and a member of the National Advisory Council. He headed a planning commission panel on rural poor and recommended rank-based system including automatic inclusion and exclusion of poor families. Dr. Saxena monitors hunger-based programs in India on behalf of the Supreme Court, and is also chairing a committee to look at the implementation of the Forest Rights Act, 2006.

Dr. Timo Voipio is Senior Advisor on Social Policy and Decent Work with the Ministry for Foreign Affairs of Finland. He can be reached at timo.voipio@formin.fi

Gowri Vijayakumar is a Ph.D. candidate in Sociology at the University of California, Berkeley. She specializes in the sociology of gender, sexuality, international development, transnational social movements, labor, and medicine, focusing on South Asia and sub-Saharan Africa. Her work has appeared in journals such as *Gender & Society* and *Global Labour Journal*.

Harsh Mander is the Director of the Centre for Equity Studies, and a Special Commissioner to the Supreme Court of India in the Right to Food case. He is a social activist and writes on issues of communal harmony, tribals and Dalits, and on disabled persons' rights, the right to information, custodial justice, homelessness and bonded labor.

ABOUT THE EDITOR AND CONTRIBUTORS

Indira Hirway is Director and professor of economics at Center for Development Alternatives, Ahmedabad, India. She has worked and widely published in the fields of poverty and human development, labor and employment, globalization and related policies, development alternatives and development paradigms, environment and development, environment accounting, gender and development, and time-use studies.

Nalini Nayak is an activist, feminist and trade unionist based in Kerala. She is associated with Protsahan in Trivandrum, and SEWA in Kerala. She is a founder member of the International Collective in Support of Fishworkers. She is the joint founder and general secretary of Self Employed Women's Association, Kerala.

Rashmi Singh is the Convener of National Forum for Action on Convergence, and President, Network and Alliance for Nonprofit Activities & Knowledge, which brings civil society, experts and government on a common platform on the issue of social inclusion and gender justice at macro level and integrated rural development at micro level. She has a distinguished track record of two decades in the government. She has received notable awards and recognitions like the Commonwealth Association for Public Administration & Management (CAPAM) Innovation awards for Stree Shakti (2006). She can be reached at rashmi.nct@gmail.com

Sejal Dand is an activist, and the founder member and director for advocacy at ANANDI, a feminist collective that works for rural tribal women in Gujarat. She is also currently a National Advisor with the Commissioner, appointed by the Supreme Court, in the Right to Food case.

Shubha Chacko is the Executive Director of Solidarity Foundation—an organization that supports sexual minorities

(LGBT) and sex workers. She has over 25 years of experience working on issues of gender, development, human rights, and social justice. She has a Masters in Social Work from Tata Institute of Social Sciences, Mumbai.

Subadra Panchanadeswaran is Associate Professor at Adelphi University School of Social Work, New York. Her area of practice and research is in the sphere of gender-based violence, specifically examining the experiences of female survivors of violence. Dr. Panchanadeswaran's research has focused on the intersections of violence, substance use and women's vulnerability to HIV. Her additional research interests include examining partner violence, issues of social support, health consequences of abuse among immigrant women in the U.S., and more recently, the impact of technology on sex workers' lives.

Subhalakshmi Nandi is the Programme Specialist for Women's Economic Empowerment in the UN Women Office for India, Bhutan, Maldives and Sri Lanka.

Yamini Atmavilas is Program Officer of Measurement, Learning and Evaluation at the Bill and Melinda Gates Foundation. She works on equity-focused evaluations, policy analysis, and gender and public health concerns, particularly around reproductive and maternal health. Adolescent health, sexuality and empowerment are her area of interest. She can be reached at yamini.atmavilas@gatesfoundation.org

About PWESCR

Programme on Women's Economic, Social and Cultural Rights (PWESCR) is a feminist human rights organization. It endeavours to promote economic, social and cultural rights, by bringing a feminist perspective to policy, law and practice at local, national, regional and international levels. It has successfully strengthened civil society voices, especially of women from poor, excluded and marginalized communities. With ever-evolving strategies and activities in both conceptual and practical realms, PWESCR has worked in partnership with various stakeholders including the UN agencies, policy makers and institutions to improve democratic governance by ensuring women's inclusion and participation.